OF LIKE PASSIONS

To Juanita Duckworth with
my blessings,
Margaret H. Gaines

Margaret Gaines

Missionary to the Arabs

OF LIKE PASSIONS

Cleveland, Tennessee

Unless otherwise indicated, Scripture quotations used in
this book are from the King James Version.

This book is gratefully
dedicated to:
Mae Jones, Margareta Poulos,
the late Beatrice Coly,
and all the Church of God
ladies they represent.

CONTENTS

FOREWORD

Margaret Gaines' story, like her life, is a gift given graciously to the sons and daughters of the Church of God. At a young age she gave herself to God, and what He has now been able and pleased to offer to the children through this one gift is simply immeasurable.

I met Margaret in 1983. She sat before me as a seminary student the first year that I taught at the Church of God Theological Seminary. Looking back now, I blush to think that I would actually try to stand before her in the role of teacher. Her grace and humility covered my naive presumption.

Just after Margaret finished my seminary course, my wife, Jean, and I invited her to our home for dinner. There at our dinner table that night I first began to encounter the chapters of Margaret's life story. I was gripped by the passion and the power of what I heard. When she finished, our table had become like an altar. I remember Margaret praying for our soon-to-arrive, firstborn daughter, and I remember her leaning forward and saying to me, with passion in her eyes, the following words that have never left me: "I believe the story I have just told you belongs to the young people of this church."

I did not realize in that moment that most of what she had just told me had been written up in a manuscript that had been submitted for publication already more than three years earlier. For some reason the manuscript had languished on some shelf, and it continued to do so for many more years.

I learned about the existence of the book only later. Margaret's concern was not so much to publish a book but to nurture children, and I was one son who had received enough of her story that I knew that it did indeed belong to the children of this church.

In a church where there are far too few elders in the true sense, where there is far too little genuine spiritual inheritance left to give to the children, Margaret Gaines and her story are like a fresh cruse of olive oil ready to be poured out on a new generation.

The original manuscript has now been augmented by an additional section in which Margaret tells the rest of her story. Reverend Douglas LeRoy and his staff are to be thanked for their crucial role in bringing this important project to completion.

Margaret Gaines, no less than Deborah of old, is surely "a mother of Israel." She is mother to many Arab children of the West Bank, where she has poured out her life. But her oil has long been spilling across all borders and anointing daughters and sons everywhere she has gone. She is no longer able to go, but this book will now go forth as a vessel to carry the touch of her oil to many more sons and daughters. It is with a sense of awesome privilege that I now say to all of them by way of commending this story, "Behold, your mother."

Rickie D. Moore
February 25, 2000

FOREWORD

(to the original manuscript)

"I press toward the mark for the prize of the high calling of God in Christ Jesus" (Phil. 3:14 KJV). I think this cry of the Apostle Paul must have been born in Margaret Gaines' soul from the time of her birth. This story, which is the story of her life, reveals that as a very young child she had keen awareness that one day she would have to commit her life to Christ forever and without reserve. As soon as Margaret made this commitment, she responded in the most literal sense to Jesus' injunction of Matthew 16:24 "If any man will come after me, let him deny himself and take up his cross, and follow me." Self-denial became the norm for Margaret's life from that point on.

Margaret Gaines' life has been marked with hardship, deprivation, rejection, loneliness, and pain, but you will find that she presents a most refreshing overview of these facts. Rather than recounting these experiences with the piteous tone so often used in similar stories, Margaret reflects on them with more of a spirit of awe at the ingenuity of God. She seems to see each negative experience as God's most cleverly designed tool to mold and shape her for the tasks to which He called her.

Insofar as the last 31 years of Margaret's ministry have been to the Arab people, it is understandable that God would have had to design a very rigorous training program properly to equip a single girl for such an assignment. However, I have never known any other individual who was so dedicated to laying down her own life that she might be conformed to the express image of Christ. Margaret chose the title *Of Like Passions* to express her sense of identification with her readers and to disclaim any special status for herself. I think the title could even more appropriately bear reference to Margaret's being *Of Like Passions* in relation to the Lord Jesus Christ, having no aim and purpose of her own, but seeking only to do the will of the Father. In her story Margaret does not present herself as a martyr, but as one especially privileged to learn obedience to the Father through the things she has suffered. I believe you will find her story a fascinating and inspiring one.

Frieda Courson

PREFACE

Those who expect *Of Like Passions*, my autobiography, to be a mission story will be disappointed in this book. It is true that I am a career missionary. It is also true that my missionary experiences were frequently cited in this narrative; however, as the title may suggest, to portray myself essentially as a missionary is not my objective. There are two reasons for this.

The first reason is that I really desire to be known as the ordinary human being that I am. Hence, you will see the candid sharing of my response to my world at varying stages in my life within the context of my Christian experience and missionary calling.

The second reason is one which I believe any reader of my autobiography will be able to see with increasing measure, as my humanity becomes more apparent. It is simply that "we have this treasure in earthern vessels so that the excellency of the power may be of God and not of us " (2 Corinthians 4:7).

In my experience, I have found too much made of the "instruments" and too little made of the Master. It may be arguable that here I have not avoided this result, given my emphasis in the following pages on my humanity. To have simply given an account of what God has done in my life would have glorified Him more. That may well be, but it has not been my purpose.

The crisis of faith which happened when I was 19 years of age just before I left Lee College in January 1951, has been treated with a minimum of detail in this story. My reason for vagueness here is that this episode is another story for another time. To have taken it up in more detail in this book would have lengthened the manuscript unnecessarily.

Likewise, the vagueness in recounting missionary experiences is because they belong to another book also. To have belabored the missionary experiences here would have been a departure from the objective.

Finally, I wish to express great appreciation for Jane Lindenborg who typed the original manuscript and who gave me pertinent advice on the nature of chapter 15.

Now, I present my story to my readers with one hope. May I become to them a woman of like passions as they, so that any honor which may come from my experiences may rightfully be attributed to the *treasures* and not to the clay pot that holds them.

Chapter 1

DEPRESSION BABY

*C*hildhood. What sensations this word evokes. Nothing in my childhood was carefree. An anonymous apprehension haunted my conscious behavior. I felt the responsibility to help protect the unknown against an unidentified danger. What was threatened? What was the threat? Was it only an illusion?

The question remains open. Founded or not, the emotion was real. Inevitably, it influenced my entire experience.

The pre-depression economic boom that swept our country did not by-pass my family. In 1921 my missionary parents returned from Japan penniless, sick and with two children — Ruth, a 2-year-old, and Paul, an infant. Their industry, thrift and adroit business ability proved to be great assets. By 1927 my mother and brother had recovered their health and three more girls — Florence, Ada and Velma — had been born to the family. My father, an accomplished building contractor as well as a pastor, had constructed his own house and had bought a 1928 Model T Ford.

The family had ample food and clothing and enjoyed modest prosperity. My father was satisfied with his pastorate of the Pentecostal Holiness Church and his musical interests. My mother, however, continually waged an ill-concealed battle. How could she harmonize her conflicting roles — missionary versus housewife? Into this setting and before the crash of the stock market in 1929, another daughter, Ollie, was born.

Before I was born in December 1931, the setting had changed dramatically. My mother, exhausted from 11 years of consecutive pregnancies and childbearing, found her duties as homemaker and pastor's wife increasingly exacting. Her health failed. Feeling guilty that she had married and "missed her mission call," she endured inner conflict without respite. To intensify her distress, the firmly established depression threatened the very existence of the family. The lean years had already devoured the fat years and were relentlessly getting leaner. The last thing the family needed was another child, especially a girl. Nevertheless, wanted or not, needed or not, I was born.

How does one support seven children in a city with no income? The perplexing problem challenged my parents' fortitude. To receive support from the ministry was out of the question. Construction was at a standstill. Although my father composed music, he was strongly opposed to selling his songs. His music was a ministry for which he refused to accept remuneration even if there were a lucrative market for musical compositions at a time when the world had nearly lost its melody. For a time, my father went from house to house, and town to town carrying a supply of spare parts and repairing stoves. It was a sensible employment. Even though there was much that people could not afford, they simply had to afford a cook stove, which not only cooked their meager meals but often served as the sole heater of the home.

The salary for stove repairs was sometimes paid in coveted cash. Usually, however, the families had no cash, so they paid with eggs or garden produce. These insufficient earnings required my father to seek other means to support his big family.

Was it weird that he decided to build caskets to sell? From today's remote perspective the idea smacks of sarcasm. Knowing my father's optimism and healthy sense of humor, I prefer to label it necessary comedy, like the humor he exhibited one day when he went to the grocery store to buy groceries. Waiting his turn at the meat counter, he covetously observed a gentleman buying lamb chops. When my father's turn came, he said to the salesman, who was a friend of long standing, "I'd like to have a piece of 'lam meat' please."

The friend, knowing my father's financial situation, responded with surprised pleasure. After disappearing briefly to the refrigerator room, he returned with a choice cut of lamb. With a mischievous twinkle in his eyes, my father exclaimed, "Oh! I regret to tell you, but that is the wrong kind of lamb. I can only afford the kind you 'lam' up against the wall to get the salt off."

Seeing comedy in life's most stressful situations was characteristic of my father. Why, then, would it be incredible to imagine that he thought, "Since survival in depression threatens to become impossible, why not use death as a means of survival?"

The casket construction business proved disastrous as a means of livelihood. Although my father built caskets from wood with beautiful cabinet-maker precision and mother covered them with velvet cloth and lined them with white silk and ribbon, he could not sell them. How could he accept pay from poverty-stricken families whose mourning tore his tender heart? He and mother agreed to give the caskets away to the needy.

But we were needy, too. My mother advanced her own plan for our survival. "Let's sell the house and buy a farm for the price of it," she suggested. "At least on a farm we could plant a garden, preserve food and raise some chickens and livestock. It would adequately sustain the family through the depression," she explained.

"But I'm not a farmer," retorted my father. "What would we feed the chickens and livestock?" "You are right," agreed my mother. "It would be a difficult enterprise. Do you have an alternative?"

No, he had none. Consequently, they traded our new house in Anniston, Alabama, for a 40-acre farm near Jacksonville, Alabama. A new era in my life began.

Chapter 2

Our Homeplace

*T*he farm, which came to be known tenderly as "the home-place," was the setting of our family's happiest years. But the farm itself had to represent something different to each family member, thereby contributing uniquely to each one's experience.

What possibly could have been my father's reaction to the farm? An enthusiastic, socially-oriented person, would he not find a farm eight miles from a small town unbearably confining? His scanty knowledge of farming coupled with the land, barren except for a network of below-surface roots and a surface accumulation of stones, spelled despair for any productivity. Felling trees to cut into kindling for selling in town and gathering wild berries and nuts for the same purpose revealed with what desperation the entire family followed him to forge an existence from nearly nothing.

From a materialistic point of view, it was a simple existence, but our family was not materialistic in outlook. Gifted with fine minds, healthy bodies, and challenged by the training of our face-up-to-a-conflict and go-down-fighting parents, we thrived on a challenge. We learned that deprivation of spirit and determination constituted the only real poverty. We learned that faith in God and the intellectual and physical potential He has given us composed the only real riches.

Yes, it was my father's face-up-to-a-conflict attitude that established his noble composure through those years and harnessed his frustration. Possibly he saw the farm as a necessary trap or prison in which he could find some means of redeeming the time. The result? He started a church in the veritable wilderness. Through it, his and my mother's needs to minister found an outlet. Exposure to people much less fortunate than we provided an excellent atmosphere in which we children could learn to identify our blessings.

My father's optimism influenced the more than 500 songs he composed. Nothing negative or sad entered his lyrics. Only praise and worship dominated his musical expressions. In the home my father organized a quartet from the family members. Everyone was taught to read music and sing. Besides his music, my father wrote poetry. One light poem he wrote simply to amuse us children.

The Man in the Moon

The man in the moon is ninety feet tall;

He weighs six thousand pounds.

His eyes are blue, his hair is green,

His complexion is chestnut brown.

His meals are poor, only one a day,
Yet they would make you laugh.
He feeds himself with a steam shovel
For five long hours and a half.

He cuts his hair with a mowing machine
Which he carries in a pack on his back.
He cleans his teeth with a grinding rock
And he clips his nails with an axe.

He sleeps very little, only naps they say,
But they are twelve hours or so.
He snuggles down in his bed of gold hay
And rocks on the wind and the snow.

If my father succeeded in converting his adversities into advantages, without ever really loving the farm, what could have been my mother's reaction?

Having enthusiastically read Madam Guyon's autobiography in her youth, my mother's philosophy was dominated by the principle of self-renunciation and annihilation which Madam Guyon so forcefully advocated. Also, the problem of survival was hefty enough to impede any mental on-slaught by all other considerations. Accordingly, Mother searched the farm not for flaws, but for favors by which it could, with God's blessing, afford her a means of providing for her children.

Mother knitted and sewed all our garments. She pieced quilts and quilted them. After our horse, Dobbin, died, she hitched herself to the plow, which she pulled while Ada or

Florence plowed her garden bed. My father (and probably Paul) never saw her do it, as he would be away in town repairing stoves, selling kindling and buying some staple goods.

Untiringly mother planted and tended her garden. Vegetables were canned for winter. From wild berries she made delicious jam which we enjoyed with her perfect yeast bread. From her strawberry bed, she and my sisters picked many baskets of berries for sale in town. Mother even made peanut butter and catsup.

While the older children were in school, my mother single-handedly carried stones and built a dam to prevent a stream, which turned into a torrent with the winter rain, from destroying the land. Working with my father, she wallpapered our house with magazines and flour and water paste to keep the draft from penetrating the unsealed frame house. Magazine wallpaper was not the fad at the time, but it provided unlimited opportunity for word games for us children in the winter.

I remember helping my mother gather a tall slender weed which she stripped and placed in the cracks between the floorboards. Afterwards she pitched them with tar. It effectively closed the cracks against bitter cold. Industrious and uncomplaining, my mother performed her tasks with an endless hymn on her lips and a prayer in her heart.

In the actual trading of our lovely city home for a farm, what were our assets?

There was a three-room house, a new barn intended for storing the harvest, an old barn that housed the livestock, and a tool house adjacent to the garage. The house was built in a right angle, with a full porch inside of the angle. One room was the kitchen; one room was the bedroom of my father, mother and Paul; and one room was the girls' bedroom. A beautiful lilac bush, a crepe myrtle bush, a bed of jonquils and two huge hickory trees beautified our front yard. This vivid memory evokes everything I know of childhood happiness and home.

I was only 18 months old when we moved to the farm, and I do not remember precisely what livestock or fowl was included in the transaction. I do vaguely remember a horse named Dobbin, that died of starvation while the family watched in helpless agony. My father was away at the time, otherwise he probably would have shot Dobbin to spare him and us the agony of his dying. But the death of Dobbin was not without the spice of comedy, especially in retrospect.

The older children dug a grave in the pasture for Dobbin's burial. After a properly conducted funeral—pastor's children are exposed to enough funerals to know how they are conducted—dear Dobbin was tenderly laid to rest in his beloved pasture. But the older children were a great deal more adept at conducting funerals than they were at digging graves. The day following the funeral, we all went to mourn at Dobbin's grave. Imagine our surprise to find Dobbin's legs, cold and stiff in death, protruding from the too-shallow grave.

I did not feel poor or deprived. I loved the farm. The family togetherness was a warm comfort in dilemma and in delight. The only sadness I can recall were things like the departure of a family member, a family quarrel or my inability to comprehend how to handle my father's admonition to "Stand on your own two feet. Do not be a burden on your world." Also, I endured poorly the distress caused by one of the children being punished for disobedience.

In the spring after we moved to the farm, mother and all the other girls went to work in the fields. Velma, then about seven years old, was left in charge of Ollie and me. She was instructed not to draw water from the well by any means. My mother left drinking water in a bucket. But

Velma eager to do a favor, used the drinking water to wash the breakfast dishes which had been left in the haste of the others going to do the planting before the rain came.

When I got thirsty and begged for water, Velma told me there was not any and I would just have to do without until our mother returned from the field. Being of an extremely independent, unpredictable and enterprising nature, I set out quietly to find water for myself. Finding what I thought was water, I drank long, but the liquid was kerosene. I lost consciousness with the bottle by my side.

Velma found me. Fearing for my life, she sent Ollie to look for mother. Velma threw me in the middle of the bed and jumped up and down on the bed screaming, "Margaret is dying! Margaret is dying!" The terrible bouncing caused by her incessant jumping resulted in my regurgitating the kerosene, and this saved my life.

When Mother came, she was relieved to find me conscious. I remember thoroughly enjoying the incident after the kerosene came up. Someone went to our neighbors and brought me fresh milk which I was allowed to drink to my heart's content. The milk was a delicious beverage of which I had never had my fill. As a bonus, Paul made me lovely dollhouse furniture and baskets out of acorns. There is a delightful side to being sick!

My father and mother were strict disciplinarians. The rules of our house were perfectly understood by every member of the family, and the punishment for disobe-dience was accepted without question. One of the rules was that everyone in our family ate together at mealtime, according to a set schedule. I usually loved to get up early and watch my parents cook breakfast, but one morning I decided to test the rule. I did not get up when I was called, although I was awake. At the last minute Ada begged me to get up and let her help me get ready for breakfast. I grunted and refused. Everyone went to breakfast while I was still in bed. I relished their resentment when Mother said it was quite alright to let me sleep. My! How spoiled I felt. I loved it!

Finally breakfast was over, and the children went to school. Mother tidied the kitchen and sat in her bedroom to mend socks. I decided to get up. After making my bed and dressing I went in to Mother.

"Good morning, Mother," I said.

"Good morning, my dear," she answered.

"I'm hungry, Mother," I said.

"That's a sign my baby is healthy," subtly replied my mother.

"I want something to eat," I advanced.

"Oh, but it is too early. Dinner is served at 12 o'clock in this house," she answered.

"But, I didn't have any breakfast," I complained.

"What a pity!" she maintained. "Breakfast is served in this house at 6:30."

Knowing that there was no use insisting, I left the room and the house fighting back tears of rage and declaring in a muted tone that I hated my mean mother. My stubbornness getting the upper hand, I devised a plan whereby I would win after all. Tiptoeing into the kitchen from the back door, I did not make as much noise as a cat. Ever so gently I lifted a chair and carried it over to the cupboard. Quietly opening the cupboard door, I took an egg, closed the door and put the chair back in its place. My mother, in the next room, heard not a sound. Then I fled to the woods. There in utter bittersweet protest, I broke the raw egg and swallowed it. Horrible! But I had proved to my satisfaction that I could win. What did I prove and to whom? The rest of my life, I never again defied a rule of the house.

Mother used to make a pallet on the floor and sit down on it with all of us children around her. So vividly she told us the Bible stories. Her concepts of God's nature of love and justice were portrayed with such living reality that I could practically see God, now smiling loving approval, now scowling a fearful rebuke.

She told us that Jesus knows everything, even our unexpressed thoughts. She told us about His first advent and the greatly anticipated second advent. "When He returns, He will take the trusting and obedient to live with Him," she affirmed. "The disobedient will remain on earth to suffer unutterable tribulation," she explained. I loved the stories, but the second coming of Christ and the terrible tribulation struck me with indescribable fear and dread, resulting in hysterical weeping. I could just envision Jesus coming and taking my family, leaving me all alone. I knew I was a sinner and would not go with Him. How I longed to tell Mother about my sin, but I hated admitting a fault. I kept silent.

It is common to overlook weighty sins of the disposition and feel guilt for superficial transgressions. No doubt, I had many sins, but the sin of which I felt convicted was stealing pickles. My mother made dill pickles in a big churn, leaving them in a walk-in closet in the kitchen. I would sneak behind the curtain, and get a pickle out of the brine, then run far away to eat it. I knew I was a thief and longed to be forgiven, but I dared not confess.

Often, while the children were in school, Mother would go to the woods to pray. When I heard her praying, I was seized with terror and could not continue my games. I would go quietly to where she was praying and listen until she finished. Once I asked her, "Mother, what were you doing?"

"I was talking to Jesus," she answered.

"Does He talk to you, too, Mother?" I asked fearfully,

wondering if He who knows everything divulged my sins. "Yes, He often speaks to me," she affirmed.

"What does He tell you, Mother?" I inquired tearfully. She never guessed the motive behind my inquiry.

Ruth and Paul, being the oldest of the children, assumed much responsibility in trying to help support the family. I scarcely recall Ruth in relation to the farm. She went to boarding school at Emmanuel College in Franklin Springs, Georgia, at a very young age. She graduated from high school and took a secretarial job for the Alabama Pipe Company in Anniston.

Ruth never thought of herself, a fact which is true to this day. She saved her earnings to buy things we needed. Once she bought a baby doll. She could afford only one so it had to be community property for Velma, Ollie and me. We had never owned a real doll. How difficult it was to share one baby among three mothers! My father would time us by the clock so we could manage, giving us 15 minutes each to hold the doll.

Ruth was instrumental in helping my father get employment at the Alabama Pipe Company. Our life-style changed perceptibly when my father began to earn a consistent salary. With the problem of survival partially solved, my mother's guilt for not being on the mission field returned to torment her. In an effort to compensate for her lost mission, she went somewhere to hold revival meetings, leaving everyone behind.

I was not yet school age. My father had no choice but to take me to work with him. Of course, he could not take me into the pipe shop with him. He left me to sit alone in the car while he worked, forbidding me to get out. The long vigil was broken only at noon when we silently ate cold biscuits and sorghum syrup. How perplexing this situation must have been for my dear father. How incomprehensible it was for me. Had my mother forsaken me forever? Had I been responsible for her departure? My fears and agonizing loneliness were smothered in silence in an effort to spare my poor father extra pain. It was the best way that I knew how not to be a burden.

After the first year's effort at farming, my father gave it up and rented our farm to our neighbors for sharecropping. They stored their cotton in our new barn. Sometimes we would play in the new barn. I loved to play with Velma and Ollie when school was out and they were at home all day. Once, late in the summer, the new barn was full of freshly harvested cotton. Also in the barn were two caskets—remnants of my father's casket construction business. One was a big, stripped casket that we used for storing black walnuts, hickory nuts and chestnuts for winter. The other was a child's casket which was not stripped. The white velvet covering and the white satin lining were beautiful. On this particular day, Velma, Ollie and I decided to play funeral. Velma was the preacher. She preached on Ezekiel and the valley of dried bones—an appropriate sermon for a funeral! Ollie was the mourner. I was the deceased. I loved being the deceased. Ollie and Velma doubled as the undertakers. They combed my hair, fixed up my face, laid me in the casket and placed my hands crossed over my heart. All the time my eyes were closed, and I lay as still as the corpse I was pretending to be. I reveled in all that attention. After the play funeral, they moaned and wailed their dramatized grief, closed me in the casket and buried me under the cotton. How realistic can a play funeral get!

In summer Velma, Ollie and I were allowed to take shower baths in the rain. How delightful was the odor of summer rain on the dust! Torrents of rain, teasingly defied all our attempts to dam it up. The stinging rain pelted our bare backs causing us to squeal with glee.

When my father changed the tires on his car, he gave us the worn out tires. With one tire we made a swing in our hickory tree. The remaining three became "cars" for Velma, Ollie and me. With hoes we traced the roads all over our yard. There were pretend roads to town, to church and to homes of our friends. Endlessly we rolled our tires making pretend conversations wherever we went.

One day, tiring of our ordinary circuit, Velma suggested that we roll our tires down the road and up a hill overlooking our house on the opposite side of the driveway. Following her in hot pursuit, we arrived breathless on the hillside. There we laid our tires down, sat in them and began to sing at the top of our voices. We sang "Everybody Will Be Happy Over There," "The Flowers Are Blooming Forever," "It Is Love," and "Oh, Our Lord Is Coming Back to Earth Again." I loved to sing, and I had memorized every song.

The repertoire included my favorites, except the last song. To refuse to sing about the second coming of Jesus would have created suspicion for which I would be called upon to divulge the reason. Therefore, reluctantly I sang, "Oh, Our Lord Is Coming Back To Earth Again" with hypocritical pleasure, when suddenly a rabbit hopped by followed by an undetermined number of hunting dogs fiercely barking. Several farmers were following closely behind shooting their double-barreled shotguns. In the commotion mixed with my hyper-imagination, I fainted from fear that the Lord had in fact come! Velma and Ollie carried me to Mother. I regained consciousness sitting on Mother's lap in our kitchen. I could hear Velma and Ollie trying to convince Mother that our neighbor had shot me. How could they ever guess what really happened?

Two mysteries perplexed me for years. One was the disappearance of a beautiful litter of kittens which our cat brought home. I loved their soft fur and amusing faces. All day I played with them. But after a night's sleep, I awoke to a mother cat's crying over her babies that had disappeared. My sorrow and keenly felt loss joined with that of the mother cat. No one ever attempted to explain to me what had happened to the unwanted kittens.

The second mystery involved a lovely dotted Swiss dress that Florence made for me. It had a plain bodice, full short skirt with a big sash, Peter Pan collar and very short puffed sleeves. The dress was finished on Saturday, ironed and hung in the doorway for me to wear on Sunday. My parents disapproved of the short sleeves and short skirt, but nothing dampened my vanity as I tried on my pretty dress and pranced in front of the mirror. Alas! When I woke up the next morning, the dress was not to be found, though we combed the house in search of it. How broken-hearted I was! No one ever revealed to me the mystery of the disappearing dress. My mother's unnatural silence could have given me a clue had I been more mature.

If my father and mother had any differences in their approach to child discipline, I never knew about it. Such a thing would have been discussed in private. To me they presented a united front. To them, having good minds, healthy bodies and faith in God's guidance and provision were ample to succeed. Therefore, all failure born of human weakness was inexcusable and unacceptable. Extraordinary achievement was treated as normal and as such merited little or no recognition. Failure to achieve extraordinarily brought down blame and belittlement. Early I got the impression that I had to achieve extraordinarily in order to justify my existence. Achievement for honor's sake did not enter my mind. Mere acceptance to life and earning a place in my world was my ever-conscious need.

No doubt Mother agreed with my father's insistence that we stand on our own two feet and be an asset to our world, with the addition of self-renunciation and annihilation as a basic principle best learned at an early age. Being a productive member of society meant more to them than simply being self-supporting and law-abiding. It implied reaching the highest possible achievement of which our minds and bodies were capable. Furthermore, "when we had done our best, we were but unprofitable servants." The "world" for me at that age was my home and family. Striving constantly not to be a burden, I tried not to need anything. Did I over-react? Did I read into my parents' training more than was intended? I admit the probability. However, if so, I see traces of the same error in my brother and sisters as though they have never learned that they are accepted as human beings by the sheer accident of being born. Human failure is forgivable and often excusable. Achievement is worthy of recognition and even praise.

How I longed to start school! I learned to print and even write long hand. I could understand number value and could quickly solve double digit addition and subtraction with borrowing and carrying over. I could read the first and second grade readers easily. But because I would not be six years old before December, I was not accepted in school in the fall of 1937. To placate me, my mother encouraged me to read the Bible to her after everyone when to school. Every time I came to a pronoun—a who, which, that, he, she or they—she would have me identify the antecedent to which the pronoun referred. It was great fun for me. I enjoyed learning with the extra bonus of experiencing my mother's rare personal attention.

When I finally went to school in the fall of 1938, I really presented a problem to the teacher. Miss Boozer had grades one, two and three in one classroom. Grades one and two did not challenge me. Constantly I interfered with grade three which was all the way across the room. As a means of coping, the principal put me up to grade two and gave me extra work. No doubt, Miss Boozer was greatly relieved when we moved to Georgia after a few weeks.

My father was called to pastor the Congregational Holiness Church in Griffin, Georgia. That meant giving up his employment at the Alabama Pipe Company. The manager promised never to employ him again no matter how great his need if he gave up his job. The church could not adequately support our family. Would my father agree to go? After much prayer and deliberation my parents agreed that it was God's will for them to accept the pastorate regardless of the cost.

The challenge of the new and unknown buoyed me up. Still, as we packed into the little car to drive to Griffin, I felt that we were leaving the best behind, never to be recaptured.

Chapter 3

GRIFFIN, HERE WE COME

*T*he past was never recaptured. In Griffin everything changed in our life-style except the basic philosophies and their dominating influence on life and discipline. Neither then nor even until now has any member of our family thrown off that influence.

We did not move any furniture from the farm. New beds from Sears Roebuck in Atlanta were waiting for us on arrival. Whether the rest of the furniture was new or whether it was used furniture provided by the church, I'm not certain. Either way, it was new to me, adding to the unfamiliarity of our new home which had three rooms. Unlike the farmhouse, it was shotgun style. We lived in it temporarily as the church soon obtained a rundown five-room house at 228 Williams Street.

My father lost no time stripping the cracked plaster from the interior of that house on Williams Street. He restored the inside walls and floors and installed a full indoor bathroom. The drab brown outside was painted a fresh white. After the renovation, I loved the new house. Restored, its original finesse reappeared.

A nice house cannot constitute a home. Home represented to my young mind the togetherness in poverty or prosperity, in amicable agreement or vehement disagreement. In our new situation, even our pleasant house could not capture and retain that wholesome togetherness that we had experienced on the farm.

Ruth, just 19, married and established her home in Anniston. Paul, still 17, finished junior college and set out for an adventurous tour of the West in search of his own identity. Florence, Ada, Velma, Ollie and I remained with our parents, but we were not together in spirit. The city provided a variety of interests. We were no longer a self-contained family. Consequently, each individual responded to the call of his or her own nature.

Florence, an attractive sweet 16, with her pug nose and vivacious personality, attracted a host of friends of both sexes. Having graduated from high school before our move, it was not a surprise when she soon married.

Ada, a homely 14, found satisfaction and much coveted recognition by being second mother. Irresistibly driven to excel as Mother's helper, she became hopelessly meddlesome and domineering. Consequently, we vindictively nicknamed her "Bossy Cow," much to our parents' distress. Blinded by her behavior, we would not get around to discovering her real values for some years.

Velma, a slightly built strawberry blond, could sing like a nightingale. Although she disagreed, I always thought she was the prettiest of the family. Comparing the two of us, I saw her as a Dresden doll while I was a dobbin horse. Needless to say, I envied her looks as well as her ability to sing so beautifully and her poise in public. To be really honest, I envied the pretty dresses, purses and other favors she frequently received from her admirers—lovely gifts which no other member of our family had ever possessed. Velma was not driven to excel. Her talents were natural and spontaneous. Her conflict was only delayed, however. She would not be spared.

Possibly Velma was naively proud. She no longer preferred the company of her kid sisters. Associating with Florence and orbiting with Florence's satellite friends absorbed her. This was facilitated by the standing rule that any older girl had to be chaperoned at all times. Velma became Florence's chaperone.

Velma thought Ollie was the prettiest one of us, though I suspect she never told her so. Unlike the rest of us, Ollie had an olive complexion. Slender and scrupulously neat and clean, she wore her modest clothes with elegant dignity. By being born and usurping her role as baby of the family, I unwittingly relegated Ollie to the most obscure, unobserved and unappreciated position in our family. Doubtlessly, she surpassed me in modesty and honesty, but no one knows it but me. By the time I was mature enough to make those observations and express them, it was too late for Ollie. She was beyond the reach of comprehending my extended heart and hand. The ability to trust love and receive it alluded her. Trapped in her anonymous role and harassed by life's enigmas and vicissitudes, she sank into a state of chaotic internal conflict which lasted the duration of her short life. Having inherited the never-give-up temperament and indoctrinated in the excel-or-cease-to-exist philosophy, she struggled to the end.

Ollie was two and one-half years my senior, a negligible difference for adults but an important difference for children. When I was an extremely childish seven-year-old, I was clutching tenaciously to my unsatiated childhood, reinforcing my grip with every admonition to grow up. The childhood, which I had never fully realized, was visibly escaping me to my famished distress.

Ollie was ten when I was seven. Satiated or not, her childhood was left behind by the magnetic and psychological attractions to adolescence. The mysteries of life itself and the search for its meaning enticed her. The answers were not available, but first hesitantly, later forcefully, the questions aroused appropriate responses. Ollie was lost to me in these responses.

What could a seven-year-old clinging hungrily to childhood possibly have in common with a ten-year-old abandoning a disappointing childhood in search of something more realistic and satisfying?

Smothered between Velma—the prematurely successful, socially sought after, pretty, talented singer—and me, plain but protected and cared for by virtue of my role as baby-of-the-family-baby-of-the-church; Ollie precociously developed an irremediable despair which she unrelentingly and savagely resisted with ever decreasing strength. She was utterly lonely as no one attended the slightest to her need or realized her undisclosed distress. Her bizarre behavior was misjudged, increasing the damage to her physical and emotional stability.

Oblivious to everything else, I was absorbed with a complex dilemma. How could I "stand on my own two feet and not be a burden to the world" and simultaneously search out and experience the adventure of childhood which I had missed? This dilemma was aggravated by the fact that my world, which was still mainly my home and family, was disintegrating. All real contact with my family was lost except, perhaps, with Ada, whose domineering manner I resisted with all the passion of my stubborn independent disposition. I experienced increasingly the loss of mother, whose role as pastor's wife claimed her. Likewise, our father was so absorbed with the care of the church; communication with him was non-existent. Compensated with an extremely optimistic and inquisitive temperament, I never despaired. What I could not control, I could hold in abeyance.

While it was increasingly difficult to claim a cozy place in my family, school compensated by fully accepting me.

The school building had been a fascinating stone mansion, part of the Grantly estate, which had been converted into a school. Not having the regimented style of architecture generally characteristic of schools, its solid structure reassured me. Did it represent something enduring in contrast to everything that was steadily changing at home? I cannot know. However, I remember finding secret, quiet comfort merely in caressing the stones of that two-story ivy-bedecked building (in comparative measure to my undivulged frustrations at home). This reassurance and acceptance was reinforced in the classroom.

In contrast to the country school, in Griffin every class was separated. Being so far ahead of Miss Boozer's second grade in the country put me in the comfortable position of intelligent high-achiever in the second grade in Griffin. There was an additional bonus. The city provided a bottle of milk for each child every day! Clearly, school became the symbol of my salvation and comfort. Forever it would have my love and loyalty.

Gradually, my world extended beyond my home and school to include the church. I was not a Christian. The guilt I had experienced since I was five years old periodically overcame me. On such occasions I would go secretly to the church or up under the house and plead with God to be patient and not destroy me, as some day I surely would "give him my whole heart forever."

Although I was not a Christian, I loved the church. The beautiful music thrilled me, though I really did not listen to preaching. Sunday school was my favorite.

My Sunday school teacher was kind and empathetic. Her husband attended another church, but he came to pick her up after the worship service every Sunday morning. This was a mystery to me. Besides our church being the best of all, his wife was such an angel that anyone could have followed her anywhere. Well, at least that was my conclusion when I was seven and eight years old.

Later, when we moved back to Anniston, my Sunday school teacher sent me my first privately owned baby doll! It was hopelessly crushed in the mail, and I never could cuddle it. My pain was analogous, though infinitely inferior in intensity, to a mother who gave birth to a stillborn child. But the loss of my baby doll did not decrease my overwhelming gratitude to my Sunday school teacher. Furthermore, it fixed forever in my memory that she was, indeed, an angel.

There was a family from Kincaid village who attended our church. Kincaid was separated from West Griffin church by about two miles of fields and woods. One Sunday I was invited to have dinner with that family. I loved to be invited. Everyone seemed to have better food than we and more of it, too. Also, being invited without my family was a new challenging experience which emphasized my self-importance. With my parents' approval, I accepted the invitation.

The food was not disappointing, and the games were great fun. That is, until the oldest girl so convincingly told me that secretly my parents had given me to them and I would never return home. I would always be her sister. I pressed her to be really truthful. She assured me that she told the truth and all the other children supported her story.

Not a word more did I add to the subject. Smilingly, quietly, hypocritically I played "Fruit Basket Turn Over" with them around the trees in the back yard while actually devising a plan of escape from this kind of adopted family.

When the children went to get a drink of water, in the pretense of waiting for them, I remained outside. As soon as they were out of sight, I fled with the speed of the driven. Leaving Kincaid village, I had the choice of crossing the main highway at Experiment Station and following the highway home. Or I could go home by a path through the ill-reputed forest and vacant fields. I feared neither. Instinctively I knew my mother would ask me which way I came. I imagined she would have more fright in retrospect if I went down the heavily traveled Highway 41 than if I came through the woods. So I chose the woods and did not reduce my speed until I fell on our front porch.

No one was at home. Had they given me away and left Griffin? Was the whole horrible story a fact? Was I to begin then and there to literally stand on my own two feet in a world which abruptly took on overwhelming proportions?

Emotions overcame reason. Immersed in the monstrous waves of fear, I scarcely heard the voice that asked me, "Are you looking for your parents? They are at a cottage prayer meeting at Mrs. Greer's house."

Hope engendered in me unanticipated strength. Leaping up without answering a word, I ran straight to Mrs. Greer's house. From a distance I could plainly distinguish my parents' voices singing "The Old Account Was Settled Long Ago." Darting in like a frightened fawn, I threw myself on the floor and buried my face in Mother's lap. Finding her was too sweet to allow my own "accounting" to threaten my joyous relief.

I did not get punished for running away. But my mother was frightened by the fact that I had returned through the ill-reputed woods—more dangerous, to her understanding, than choosing the well-traveled highway. Perplexed, I quietly accepted her reasoning. All of my life my logic has been the opposite to what I expected the norm to be.

A family having three boys attended our church. Once the parents left the boys in my mother's custody while they were away. Apparently the discipline in their family had not been as rigid as in ours. My mother would not bridge the defiance of a child in her custody.

To my horror the middle son disobeyed my mother. Adding affront to injury, he defied her. Since his background was different from my own, I am certain he did not grasp the gravity of his actions as I did. The beating that I would have expected from my mother under the same conditions was not spared him. Since he was adverse to repenting, I thought my mother would beat him to death. Maybe he finally thought so too, as he repented and to my great relief Mother stopped beating him.

The beginners' class in our Sunday school was called the Sunbeams. At Christmas the church provided a sack of treats for every member and a special gift for the Sunbeams. Christmas 1938, the Sunbeams received a small set of porcelain kitchen furniture. I was so absorbed by the joy every child expressed that I completely forgot I was a Sunbeam. Two of the sets were left over so they were given to the youngest members of the next class. I realized that I had not received one. Probably, I never expected "things" for myself. Seeing people happy and united constituted the greatest joy of my life. I never missed the furniture nor even regretted that I did not get one.

One day mother was cooking macaroni and cheese for dinner. A small amount of cheddar cheese was waiting on the table to be put into the macaroni. I passed through the kitchen and saw the cheese. The sight of the delicious cheese paralyzed my power to reason. I forgot that we did not eat between meals or take anything without asking. I forgot that provisions in our household were so meager that my taking a generous taste of the cheese would deprive the entire family of cheese for their macaroni. Yielding to temptation, I took a generous taste.

It did not take a detective for my mother to find out that I was the culprit. My paralyzed power of reason was immediately restored. In anticipation, the blows of the leather could already be felt stinging my legs. Worst of all, the full impact of my entire family being deprived of cheese hit me. The realization that I was definitely an unsupportable burden on my world crushed me. How I longed for the deserved beating as it alone would help compensate my terrible debt.

Mother did not beat me. Why? Could she see all the real penitence in my face and understand my distress? Could she understand the injustice of beating a half-starved child for taking cheese that had been temptingly left exposed to view? Was it simply that she was weary of disciplining children? Was it a combination of all these? I do not know. But my lesson was learned without the beating. Forevermore, I thought before I ate.

No matter how poor we were, my parents simply would not abide the suggestion of going on welfare.

There was a Pirkle family in our community that was as big as ours. They went on welfare. I never recalled a single member of our family discussing them. Perhaps they understood and accepted the facts with solicitude. How I longed to ask someone, anyone, if they were still worthy of being alive or if they were outcasts and their lives threatened. Surely to be on welfare implied that they were not standing on their own two feet and they were a burden on their world. What could be a more dreadful situation? I did not dare open my mouth to ask. Silently, I pitied them.

A little before Christmas 1939, I was getting a quilt from the closet when I found hidden among its folds dolls, balls, marbles and toy cars. I could hardly wait till Christmas. I expected to receive the beautiful toys. It would be the first Christmas in my entire eight years to receive toys. The anticipation was nearly more than I could contain. But contain it I would, or how could I ever explain what could seem like "snooping?"

Christmas came, and the toys all disappeared from

their hiding place and from our house. Later, I learned that they were toys the welfare had provided for the Pirkle children. They were generous enough to give me one of the dolls. It was a girl doll with stiff legs and a green checked dress with a bonnet to match. I was glad to get the doll but not without serious reservations. The immediate most tangible, though unexpressed, objection was that I loved baby dolls that I could cuddle, feed and change the diapers. How could I relate to an inanimate stiff-legged girl doll? These emotions were much too ungrateful to be expressed.

My intangible objection was born out of my chaotic, distressing problem of deciding how to understand and accept the Pirkles being on welfare and to what extent I would be personally implicated in their situation by accepting the doll. I longed for help in sorting out my thoughts and emotions, but I found no one with whom I felt the liberty to discuss it.

In the vacant fields between our neighborhood and Kincaid village were many hog pens. One day I meandered off to the fields to see the hogs. While I was there, I saw a hog that had escaped from its pen. Intending to return it to its pen, I chased it. Some boys saw me and said it was forbidden to chase hogs because they would die if they ran. They promised to go right then and notify the police of what I had done.

Immediately, I ran home. The remainder of the day I sat pensively on our porch in fear and dread anticipating the arrival of the police. How would I ever explain my guilt to my parents and compensate for the shame I had brought on them? Had I not been too independent, I could have discussed it with my mother and spared myself much anguish. Instead, I hid the matter until I went to bed. I could not sleep. Late into the night, trembling and icy cold, I slipped out of bed and went to Mother. Out came the whole story. She reassured me, admonished me, and told me to go to sleep. All was well.

On Sunday, August 25, 1940, my mother requested the opportunity to tell the church something. Standing in the choir, she bade the whole church goodbye. "I have enjoyed working with you wonderful people for these two years," she began. "Now, I must inform you this will be the last service I shall attend in this church. In the coming week I shall go home to heaven. Either the Lord will come for us all, or He will simply call for me. I am ready. Goodbye, dear friends," she concluded. Then she sang "Jesus, Lover Of My Soul."

There was a great commotion in the congregation and many wanted to pray in the altar. Did they believe what she said? She was not apparently ill. Maybe the Lord was going to come. My mother's life usually gave credence to her word, but this whole story was too dramatic to accept without some proof.

My father left early Monday morning, taking Ada and Ollie with him for a previously scheduled revival in Sylacauga, Alabama. All day Monday I went with Mother visiting every church member who was not in church on Sunday. Joyfully, Mother announced to each one what she had told the assembly on Sunday.

Tuesday, Mother was too ill to get out of bed. A group of ladies met at our house. When they saw Mother in excruciating pain with an extraordinarily extended abdomen, they began to fear the worst. All their attempts to treat her failed, so they decided to unite in prayer until God sent my father home.

In Sylacauga, my father felt urgently that he had to close the revival and return to Griffin that same night. After the close of the service, my father took Ada and Ollie and drove the six hours without food or rest.

Arriving in the driveway, my father said, "Ada, there is something seriously wrong with your mother."

"Maybe not," she answered, trying to assure him.

"Yes, I know there is" he retorted. "In all my married life, I have never once returned home expected or not, without finding her waiting and watching at the window." With that remark they entered the house. The ladies were still praying for God to send my father home. With his arrival, they left Mother in his care and returned to their homes.

It was late Wednesday afternoon when the doctor finally came to our house. He gave Mother some medicine and promised to return the following morning. My mother could not hold anything on her stomach, not even the medicine. When the doctor returned the following day, he had her hospitalized and prepared for emergency surgery.

We were all waiting in the hospital entrance just before she went into surgery. The doctor came out of a door at the end of the hall and came to us. Florence and Ada asked him about my mother. He said he had just left her side. That was my cue. While they were absorbed in this discussion, I darted down the hall to the room from which I had seen the doctor come.

There was my mother. Her abdomen was greatly distended. A tube was down her nose. Her face was ghastly white. She saw me and spoke.

"Dear child, don't be afraid or sorrowful. Mother is going home to see Jesus today. It's beautiful in His house. You just get prepared to come and see me there someday," she said.

I did not have time to answer, even if my emotions had allowed it. The doctor came to take her to surgery. He rushed me out, as an eight-year old was forbidden in the wards.

At 2 o'clock on Thursday afternoon, August 29, 1940, Mother answered the call to go home to Jesus. Practically all that remained of home and family died with her. The adventure of childhood passed with one tragic blow.

Stunned, lost, I sank into silence to wait.

There were two funerals, one in Griffin and another in Anniston. The church in Griffin was filled, and many cars joined the funeral cortege for the long drive to Anniston. There was no room for the visitors or flowers from Griffin at the church in Anniston. The friends of my parents packed the second church, leaving room only for Mother's casket and the family. As the afternoon shadows lengthened, we left Mother's body to rest in Edgemont Cemetery.

The family returned home in search of the pieces of our shattered life.

Chapter 4

$\mathcal{H}$OLDING $\mathcal{L}$IFE IN $\mathcal{A}$BEYANCE

O ur family had come to more than a crossroads—a major intersection at rush hour typifies the situation better.

After Mother's funeral we never returned to Griffin as a family. The older girls helped my father pack up to move and attended the last services at the church. Ollie and I stayed with Ruth until my father moved.

Being in shock from Mother's sudden death, penniless and facing the opening of a school year with four children still in school, and nowhere to go placed us squarely in the traffic jam. Mrs. Hillman, a longtime friend of my parents, offered my father a store where we could stay temporarily. It was situated in a rough part of town. With no available alternative, he accepted the kind offer and utterly humiliating circumstances with grace and forbearance.

A curtain partitioned the store, making two small rooms. There was no plumbing in the building and rats infested the place. I remember peeking out between curtains and overhearing two black ladies discussing our family and describing us as "white trash." I did not know what "white trash" was, but I felt that our dignity had been overlooked. For the first time I questioned myself as to whether or not I overlooked the dignity of black people simply because they were underprivileged.

In September 1940 employment was not available to a middle-aged man. Taking the last step down to the very bottom of desperation and humiliation, short of going on welfare, my father returned to the Alabama Pipe Company to apply for a job. The manager kept his word never to hire my father again regardless of his need.

Ollie and I started to school at Pine Avenue Elementary. Velma and Ada went to Anniston High School. Daily as a family we knelt and prayed for God to provide our needs and give our father employment. True to our basic philosophy, each one of us mentally tabulated our needs and reduced them to the strictest essentials to relieve the burden.

My father accepted the call to pastor the Congregational Holiness Church in Sylacauga. Sunday mornings early we would go to Sylacauga, stay all day attending morning and evening services, then drive back to Anniston late Sunday night. I still shiver at memories of waking up in a warm car, going out into the cold midnight and going into our cold house and to cold beds.

Every Sunday some church member would invite us to dinner and supper. The church would give us a good food offering, but I think the cash offerings barely paid for my father's travel expense.

Having reached bottom, my father refused to lie there and pine away. Spurred on by his honor and dignity, he decided to redeem his time by building his family a house. Assessing his potential, he had building skills, a good reputation and unshakable faith in God.

He bought a lot at 2415 Moore Avenue. He then went to the lumber company and acquired enough lumber on the word of his honor to build the house. Bare handed through the cold winter months he constructed a lovely home. When it was completed in the spring, we moved out of the store physically and out of the pit mentally.

Against this setting I entered fourth grade. I had nothing under control. Since I last saw my mother in the hospital, I had not shed a tear, and I had spoken as little as possible. While I definitely was not in despair, I was holding everything in suspension until I could re-activate my mind to handle my emotions. Though I was stunned beyond the power to grasp any of life's loose ends, it was not betrayed to any of my contemporaries. The pent-up poison of total anguish could not pierce my shell of silent composure, but it did erupt in boils all over my body.

Dear, stable, motherly Ada lanced my boils. But I had one huge carbuncle on my left arm which only a doctor could handle. My father took me to Doctor Watson who lanced it while I watched with stoic self-control, not making a sound. This behavior, which seemed normal to me, amazed the doctor. My father recounted the story to Ruth later in the day.

"What did the doctor give you for being so patient?" Ruth inquired.

That was the first time in my life I could remember hearing it suggested that patience would be recognized or rewarded. Astonished by the mere suggestion, I blurted out, "Nothing!"

"Well, you should have gone to my doctor. He gives children a piece of fruit or some candy when they are that patient," she affirmed.

Learning from my loss, I programmed my mental computer with that exciting tidbit. Either fruit or candy, it did not matter; they were equally loved and equally rare.

Very shortly after that conversation, when nine boils broke out on my left arm and eight on my right simultaneously, my father started to take me back to Doctor Watson. Not surprisingly, I staged a firm protest. I wanted to go to Ruth's doctor.

My stubbornness prevailed. Ollie and I went alone to Ruth's doctor. Again I bore the agonizing pain with forbearance, buoyed up with the hope of getting a piece of fruit or some candy. When the trial was over and I had passed brilliantly, I did not receive any candy or fruit! Never did I mention it, but trying to sort out the philosophical why was more painful than the mere loss of a reward. Did Ruth tell me a lie? Was it unworthy of me to have anticipated a reward? Was it simply that an eight-year-old is not a child?

Halloween had passed, Thanksgiving Day was approaching, and I still had not broken through my silent grief. About this time, I was distracted in class and did not respond when my teacher spoke to me. She called me up to her desk and whipped my palms with a ruler. I had never been whipped in school before. Immediately the floodgates of uncontrollable tears flew open. The reservoir of pent-up grief with gasping sobs shook my body, and try as I would, I could not stop it. My poor teacher, ignorant of my interior conflict was unaware of the fact that when she whipped my hands her action symbolized a far weightier act. She ridiculed me in front of the class for crying like a baby for such a small thing.

To me it was no small thing. The beloved school was my comfort and salvation, my sole escape from the mental and emotional harassment of my whole complicated life situation. Now, to my childish mind, the school had rejected me. I had become burdensome to this last bright spot in my world. My entire universe dissolved and poured out with my tears. I despaired at last! I fear to imagine what would have been my end had not two beautiful events happened then to restore my optimism.

One Sunday in Sylacauga, a lovely childless couple implored my father to give me to them. They loved children. They were devout Christians, and they were financially affluent. They had loved my mother. They promised to take as good care of me as my father would.

I watched my father's face. Torn by the realization that they possibly would take better care of me than he could ever hope to, he probably wondered if he were doing me an injustice by refusing. "I cannot give my baby away," he finally answered triumphantly. "I may not be able to provide for her as well as you could, but you cannot love her as well as I can. I'll never abandon my children so long as I have the power to keep them," he added.

What balm! My father loved me and would not give me away. He had never known how to express it, except in work. But this was a definite confirmation of his love to which I would cling all my life.

What bliss! I was not an intolerable burden on my world after all. My father had an excellent chance to rid himself of me and he did not. I preferred poverty with my father who loved me over beautiful clothes, toys and a lovely home with a couple who may tire of me.

The second event happened on my birthday, December the second. Mrs. Hillman baked me a birthday cake. She carefully decorated it with garlands of roses and put nice candles on it, while I watched in rapturous admiration. Never before in my life had I had a birthday cake! Suddenly, my fortune was too great to contain. I was beside myself with delight. Restored, I knew somehow I would get life's pieces back in place. My long tragic night would end. I could detect the promising lights of dawn already.

OF LIKE PASSIONS

My father mortgaged the finished home, thereby paying for the material he had bought to build it. Ruth moved
into the new house with us. She worked, and her salary
helped sustain us, as my father still had not found
employment. It was a happy time for me. A portion of our
family regathered. The faces looked brighter, and the voices were more relaxed, in spite of numerous problems still
lurking behind the scenes.

Our new house was pretty and comfortable. We had
ample supplies of boiled vegetables and corn bread, so we
did not miss the meats and desserts. Old Kate, a wise,
devoted Christian black woman, came daily to cook and
take care of Norman, Ruth's son, until we got home from
school. My father co-contracted a construction job, which
provided him with hope and sustained his dignity. Thus
the spring and summer of 1941 was a happy time for me.

Unfortunately, it did not last. Ruth moved to Texas in
the summer of 1941 initiating a renewed break-up of the
family. My father's construction job was nearly completed. Occasionally, he would take us for a ride to the most
affluent residential section of town to show us the beautiful brick house he was building. Returning from these
rides, he assured us that when the house was finished and
he got paid, he would buy us some shoes and dresses.
Every Saturday I would ask him if he got paid. One day he
said, "Next Saturday I'll be paid. Be ready to go to town in
the evening to get some new clothes."

Most of the summer I had gone barefoot. My shoes
from the last spring had big holes in the soles. My hand-
me-down dresses were hopelessly too small. How I joyfully anticipated the coming Saturday.

But my father did not come home Saturday afternoon.
It was late Saturday night when he arrived home. His
shoulders were stooped. He had visibly been crying.
Instinctively, I realized something had gone wrong, so I
refrained from asking any questions. Nevertheless, he

52

apologized saying, "I'm sorry you are disappointed. I finished the job, but I'll not get paid. There was a miscalculation in the number of bricks needed for the house because it was built on a hill instead of flat land. The difference in the cost consumed my whole pay for the job. There will be no shoes yet."

My disappointment was real. But his disappointment and heartache were overwhelming. His soaring hopes crashed with a deafening roar; then silence hauntingly shouted, "What will you do now? Where will you go from here?" All the months of strenuous unrequited toil pressed on him from behind. The future offered no immediate hope for a change of circumstances. To intensify the agony, his family looked to him for the evasive answers. Also he owed the mortgage on the house with no means to pay. How did he maintain his equilibrium? How many reverses could one man endure alone? How did he not despair and put us in an orphans' home? With mature judgement far beyond my years, I could assess something of his plight, making it easier for me to resign to the situation. But I realized the source of his amazing fortitude the following morning when I awakened to his singing:

Let the stormy breezes blow

Their cry shall not alarm me.

I am safely sheltered here

Protected by God's hand.

Here the sun is always shining

Here there's naught can harm me.

I am safe forever

In Beulah Land.

Dwelling in Beulah Land by Charles Austin Miles, 1911

God was truly my father's Helper. But I wanted to help him, too. What could I, nearly ten years old, do to ease my father's load? I could be obedient and try not to need anything. I could do my best in school to honor his name.

Armed with these resolutions, I reinforced my efforts to compensate to him all I could. I obeyed to the best of my understanding, and my grades were excellent in school. If my clothes were hopelessly inadequate, I never voiced a need for anything new.

Five days following my birthday in December 1941 came the shattering news that the Japanese had bombed Pearl Harbor, dragging the United States into World War II. No one knew all the implications of that announcement. Everyone knew that life would never be the same again whatever happened.

Immediately, everybody and everything was mobilized for the war effort. My father was employed at the Ordinance Depot where he worked 16 hours every day except Sundays. Within five months Ada and Velma married and left Anniston. Ollie and I remained alone. Ollie had her personal interests and friends. That kept her occupied. I rarely saw her except at night. Also, she spent the summer of 1942 in Texas with Ruth. That left me alone.

On the end of our block lived two girls with their parents and grandparents. The father and mother worked, leaving them in their grandparents' care.

Being a very early riser habitually, I had time to get up, clean up the house, eat breakfast and get bored long before my friends got up. Usually I would go down the street and sit on a bridge outside their yard to watch patiently for their venetian blinds to open. Finally, they would come out to play. Every day I would play with them from the time they got up until they went to bed. Only at mealtime would I go home. Looking back, I wonder at the patience of that grandmother. Although I stayed out of their house and I never ate a meal there, I imagine my presence grew tiresome to her many times. No doubt, my playing there protected me from dangerous exposure on the streets of our city, especially since Anniston was the location of Fort McClellan.

My father started dating a beautiful widow. She had jet-black hair, crystal royal blue eyes and complexion as smooth and white as cream. She stood tall and erect and wore clothes in excellent taste. It was apparent my father loved her. When I was nearly twelve years old, he married her. I could not call her mother, but I was so pleased we were going to have a home again. For weeks before she came I imagined how wonderful it was going to be. I would love her and accept her. I would tease her playfully, but I would respect her.

Finally, the day came when my father brought her home. Ignorant child that I was, I did not know how to articulate my pleasure that she was there. It should have been evident from my facial expression, so intense was my feeling. My awkward words insufficiently expressed my feelings. When I finally made an effort to tease her by saying playfully, "Come on, let's box." She looked at me with dignified horror. She whirled around and went straight to the bathroom without a word. Extremely perplexed, I wondered if she had become suddenly ill and if I could do anything to help her. She stayed in the bathroom for an hour. My father had gone to get his riders from work. Ollie was not there. I was alone and frightened. When she finally emerged from the bathroom, I asked her if she were ill and could I do anything for her. She pushed me aside and disappeared into her bedroom saying, "I never dreamed that Mr. Gaines' children would want to beat me the first night I entered his house." She refused any explanation. Astounded, I stood gaping, concluding that I certainly would have to handle this beautiful woman like the fine crystal doll she resembled.

Mama Floyd, as I called her, loved my father very much. She obviously took pleasure making him a spotlessly clean house, delicious meals and caring for his clothes. Pride and pleasure made her face even more beautiful. In retrospect, I understand that she tried to communicate with me. She never ever beat me or even quarreled with me, but when she was upset, she would withdraw for days, not speaking to anyone. No one ever knew who upset her, so everyone suffered the distress without discussion until she got over it. No doubt, in her own mind, what we interpreted as pouting, she thought was patience and endurance of what could very well have been extremely difficult circumstances. Probably my own fearful withdrawal and my effort to make myself as unobtrusive as possible constituted one of her worst trials. Could I have been a normal child, freely expressing my good and bad traits, she could have coped with me better.

My quiet coexistence with Mama Floyd contrasted Ollie's outright rebellion, which rapidly degenerated into hatred. Mama Floyd could never have guessed the very real deep-rooted emotions that dictated Ollie's reactions. She did not have the wisdom to comprehend and cope with the challenge. Consequently, all her dealing with Ollie and her relationship with my father concerning her, pushed Ollie past the point of no return. Ollie's faith in God and man was shattered in the ruins of her own self-esteem. Although she would struggle many more years to reconstruct her life, she never succeeded. Helplessly, I observed what was happening, but I was too immature to sort the data and draw appropriate conclusions. My rare efforts to defend Ollie were misinterpreted, making matters worse for her. Finally, I gave up trying, but I did not give up caring.

For two years we lived in this state of increasing tension and decreasing comprehension. My internal conflict reached explosive proportions. Then came a drastic change.

On January 16, 1946, I went to the woods near our house to find an escape. The beautiful quiet forest offered me a healing retreat. Sitting on a fallen log, shivering with the winter's cold, I spotted something squirming in the stump of the log. Rising to investigate, I found a family of opossums. The mother had been shot and had dragged her bleeding body home to her babies before she died. The restless, starving youngsters struggled to find the warm, sustaining milk that her stiff body could no longer provide. Helpless and deeply shaken, I identified with the orphaned opossums. Absorbing their problem into my own over-burdened heart, I began to sob out my desolation. Hours later when my well of tears ran dry, I began to reflect on life and death. My reflections culminated in this little verse:

Death

What is this ghastly ghost I see?

What is this figure approaching me?

Is death calling me to rest?

Have I lived my very best?

Have I done everything I could?

Could I do more if I would?

Could I live a better way?

If only I would kneel and pray?

If death's angel be near to me

And I shall cross over the sea

Before I go I want to say,

Please, live your best in your future day.

OF LIKE PASSIONS

But I had never knelt to pray except to beg God to be patient with me. Surely, if I wanted to be prepared to live or to die, I needed the Savior with me. What was I waiting for? Why had I not given Him my heart?

I had wanted to have some fun first. In my mistaken concept, most, if not all, fun was sin. Once I gave my life to God I never ever wanted to go back. I had kept God waiting, begging for His patience since I was five years old. In that nine years I had had everything except fun. My chances of experiencing fun in the future seemed remote. I did not want to keep God waiting forever. What did Solomon say? He, the wisest and mightiest man of his day, spared neither might nor money in exhausting all the pursuits of pleasure known to man. He concluded, "It is all vanity." Well, I could never hope to push my research for pleasure as far as Solomon did. If I were a little wise, I would accept his conclusion. Then and there I made a proposition to God. "Lord," I prayed, "if you spare my life until tonight, I'll go to the revival and give you my heart without reserve and without return."

The remainder of the day I waited with conscious relief that one great conflict of my life was reaching an end. That night at the Sixteenth Street Church of God in Anniston, Alabama, I made my total dedication to God. Unexpressible relief rushed into my aching soul. A sense of belonging, previously unknown and unexpected, quietly enfolded me. Unutterable peace embraced me. Never again would I cope with life alone.

The following night I was baptized in the Holy Spirit. Immediately, He began comforting me, instructing me, and shaping me. The Spirit awakened in me an avidity for Bible study. I discovered the values of prayer. My spiritual nuptials to my Lord consummated my joy. For months a profound solemnity enthroned me.

The church became my world. In it I found opportunities to serve, and I served in many types of ministries.

My brother, who had recently returned from military service overseas, also returned to God at the same time. He made plans to attend Bible Training School. Influenced by his decision, I made application to the Academic Division and was accepted. The faithful Guide to whom I had trusted my life was preparing to open to me undreamed of horizons.

Chapter 5

HE DIDN'T TURN ME DOWN

A rude awakening awaited me on the steps of the administration building of the Bible Training School (B.T.S.) when I arrived. Even more startling was the surprise that engulfed me when I saw my dormitory room. The splendid ivy-bedecked towers and massive stone arcades, the stately trees shading the campus and the cozy dormitory rooms—all products of my fantasy—faded in the stark reality.

Having arrived three days early, I found only several staff members. There was no welcoming committee to initiate greenhorns like me. The dormitory rooms wore the accumulation of three months' dust on their stacked up furniture. Then and there I learned a valuable lesson: Give the imagination freedom to construct delightful and refreshing situations without neglecting mental down-toearthness that buffers the inevitable shock of landing in reality.

I would have two roommates, I was told. With time on my hands, I determined to prepare a happier reception for them than I had received. I cleaned and arranged the room and displayed a bright "Welcome" sign. When the students began arriving, I acted as self-appointed welcoming committee to the bewildered, even while my natural shyness restrained me from speaking to the obviously initiated.

I loved B.T.S. from the beginning. The big family atmosphere with President E.L. Simmons acting more like a father than a president fulfilled my personal needs. The plain, adequate food pleased me, while the routine provided constructive, organized activity with opportunities for self-expression.

My brother, who had arrived at B.T.S. earlier than I, was employed by the maintenance department. His duties kept him occupied, so he could not spare the time to take a planned trip to Newfound Gap in the Smokies. He gave me two round-trip tickets and told me I had only one day more before official opening of school. If I could find someone to go with me to the mountains before the official opening, I had better do it, because afterwards we would need a chaperone to make the trip.

Losing no time, I prevailed upon my roommate, Lois, to go with me the following day. Although she was several years my senior, I had more initiative, so she willingly trusted me to guide. Fortunately, she ignored that I knew nothing about it.

Our first mistake was miscalculating the difference in temperature on the mountains in contrast to the valley. Our light sweaters, inadequate by day, left us pathetically exposed after sundown. Our second mistake was staying at Newfound Gap until sundown.

Thinking that we had plenty of time, Lois and I let the

first returning bus go by. We attempted to catch the second bus, but it was overloaded and would not stop for us. A third bus, which was due before sundown, broke down before it reached Newfound Gap. The other visitors quickly left. Lois and I were alone except for a forest ranger parked at a distance. We felt secure as long as we could see him.

The penetrating chill and the fear of bears preoccupied us until a carload of drinking men arrived and parked near the forest ranger. Lois and I stared down the mountain, mentally pleading for the bus to come and simultaneously praying that the men, who by then had spotted us and were making quasi-complimentary remarks, would stay away. Finally, an elderly couple arrived and stopped their car to get water. Boldly, I asked them to take us to Gatlinburg and confessed our imprudence. They complied and took us, to our tremendous relief.

From Gatlinburg we soon got a bus to Sevierville. Arriving at B.T.S. around 10 o'clock in the evening, we considered ourselves exceedingly fortunate that we returned safely and that no one asked us any questions.

From this experience I learned a second important lesson: Self-confidence is valuable only as it is tempered with prudence.

The first week in December the Mission Club sponsored Mission Week. The World Missions Board was present to interview prospective missionaries. Among other outstanding speakers was Miss Josephine Planter, a veteran missionary to Tunisia. She spoke of the extremely rare missionary activity for Arabs. She emphasized that she was 79 years old and had no one to relieve her or replace her, and she appealed for volunteers to answer God's call to the Arabs.

All week I could not escape that message. On Sunday night, December 6, 1946, following Reverend Lemon's message, I responded to the call to pray for missions. Rushing to the altar, I pleaded with God to send out missionaries. After I prayed a long time I detected more resonance than penetration in my supplication. I stopped and quietly listened to God. He spoke to my inner being: "You have no right to ask that others be sent unless you give me the chance to turn you down."

"Oh, God," I volunteered, "if I'm fit material for the mission field, do please send me."

He did not turn me down. He assured me that I was His chosen representative to the Arabs.

Exploding with the need to share my joy that God had called me, I walked out of the auditorium to find my brother at the water fountain nearby. "Oh, Paul," I exclaimed. "God has called me to the Arabs."

"Oh, no. Not you!" he replied. "You will never be able to survive as a missionary to Arabs unless you have a double portion of God's Spirit."

Immediately, I realized that spiritual experiences and revelations could not be shared indiscriminately. I resolved not to speak of my call again.

Grieved by his incredulity, I, nevertheless, remained undaunted. He only sparked in me the determination to receive a double portion of God's Spirit.

What is a double portion of God's Spirit? I'm as ignorant now as I was then as to what it is exactly or if it is indeed a legitimate request. But if Paul said it was a prerequisite for survival as a missionary, I knew no better place to seek it than from God.

Secretly, I pleaded with God to give me the coveted blessing.

"God," I bargained, "I'll fast 24 hours if you will give me a double portion of your Spirit."

Probably unimpressed with the bargaining attitude, God let me try to fast 24 hours with no help from Him. Somewhat proudly, I managed it for 22 hours, then I was tempted and drank water. Stricken by my failure, I allowed Satan to buffet me.

"Look at this prospective missionary who proposed to suffer every kind of hardship and affliction on a mission field," he derided. "You can't even fast for 24 hours. Suppose you had no food on that mission field for 24 days. What would you do?" he challenged.

I could not, would not answer Satan, but I was too embarrassed to talk to God. Estranged from God, I was lonely and lost my joy. I could not endure that estrangement more than a week. Returning to God, I implored Him, "Please, restore to me the joy of my salvation. I repent of the presumption that I could fast for 24 hours. I confess that I could never endure the stresses of the mission field without supernatural help."

Waiting helplessly in prayer, I felt definitely led to fast without food or water for a week. "What?" I questioned God. "You know I failed to fast one day. I cannot fast a week. But I'll promise to fast hour by hour as long as you help me."

Supernaturally, I was sustained as I fasted. I experienced neither hunger nor tiredness. On the third day, my roommates begged me to break the fast. I explained that I could not and I asked them please not to disclose to anyone that I was fasting. On the fourth day, however, they informed Margareta Poulos, my dormitory supervisor, that I had not been to meals in four days.

The following morning Margareta posted a note on the bulletin board for me to report to her office. Suspecting the reason for the summons, I deliberately postponed reporting to her office as long as I could without arousing suspicion. She asked me if it were true that for five days I had not gone to meals. I confessed that it was true and gave her the requested explanation. She tactfully pointed out that a 15-year-old, growing girl needed good nourishment, especially if she desired the health to be a missionary. She asked me to be really careful and prayerful and not be deceived. She advised me to return to meals the following day. I expressed appreciation for her concern, and I promised to pray.

Going into the lounge of Mimosa Hall, I prayed, "Father, you have sustained my strength and courage in this fast. You are still helping me. How can I break my promise to fast as long as you are helping me? What shall I do about the people?"

"Obey me and do not heed anyone," He answered, filling my cup to overflowing.

Leaving this quiet place, I resolved to avoid Margareta the rest of the week.

On the sixth day Paul sent word for me to come see him. Knowing why he called me, I postponed seeing him also until late afternoon. As I walked into the apartment where he and his wife lived, he greeted me saying, "Look at yourself. You are a skeleton! What do you have to say for yourself concerning this fast?" He paused, and I remained silent. "Well," he continued. "You have until tomorrow noon to decide to go eat. If you continue this fast I'll go to Anniston tomorrow and tell Papa that you have lost your mind and he must come and take you out of school." I answered that if that was all he wanted I would go. Leaving Paul, I went back to the prayer room.

"Oh, God!" I prayed. "You have heard Paul's threat. I do need to stay in Bible School if I want to go to the mission field. You are still helping me, and I want to obey you. What shall I do?"

"Obey me and do not fear threats," He replied, comforting my spirit.

Then, I decided to resort to some ruse. Customarily, the different divisions of B.T.S. would alternate going first in the cafeteria line. Observing that the religious education division was heading the line and the high school division was taking up the rear, I planned to go to the cafeteria and pretend to eat. Happily, as I entered the cafeteria, Paul and his wife were leaving. I expected my ruse to work. I ignored the fact that by that time I was in an arena, so to speak, and the entire student body was quietly wondering what I was going to do. These observers reported to Paul that I did not eat or drink. Furiously, Paul drove to my father's house to carry out his threat.

When Paul was speaking to my father about 9 o'clock in the evening, I was in chapel. Even in chapel I ignored the fact that the entire student body was solidly behind me, praying for my victory. A spirit of dryness and near rebellion assaulted me. I did not want to pray. I could not sense God's presence. The fear of having to leave school assailed me. Self-pity swept over me. Probably, I could have left the auditorium without experiencing my blessing had not Faye Gleason come to me and said, "At least go to the altar and receive what God has in store for you."

In the altar I could not pray. Mrs. Nina Driggers, my English teacher, gently said, "Margaret, say thank you, Lord, for the blessing."

"Thank God for what blessing!" I thought. "Is it a blessing to long for something, obey God and as a result only be withdrawn from school?"

"Thank God for the blessing," she quietly insisted.

Then, I thought ungratefully, "It's a little thing to do, and at least it will satisfy Sister Driggers." So without faith or feeling I said, "Thank you, God, for the blessing." Instantly a bolt of power struck me, knocking me prostrate. Wave after wave of glory flooded me. I was conscious only of His silent love. When I could finally speak again, I most gratefully exclaimed, "Thank you, God, for the blessing." Again a bolt of power charged me, transporting my spirit to inexpressible realms of light. After a third time experiencing the formidable power in response to my thanks, I feared to express my thanks again, because I could not physically endure the tremendous power.

Paul found my father in bed. He told him everything that I was doing. My father got up and would have left immediately to take me out of school. Then Mama Floyd said, "Why should you lose a night's sleep? If you leave here now, what time will you arrive in Sevierville? You will have to wait hours before you can go to B.T.S. Why not wait and go in the morning?" He heeded her and waited, but by morning God had changed his mind. He never mentioned it again.

My father paid my tuition and board at B.T.S., but he ignored all my personal expenses. It was my responsibility to tell him what I needed and expect him to provide it. My inflexible independence undermined my ability to ask. I preferred to do without anything I could not earn. Local residents often called B.T.S. for temporary help with ironing, cleaning or baby-sitting. Taking advantage of these opportunities, I did earn enough usually to buy notebook paper, pencils and personal incidentals.

Once, however, I had to write a research paper, but I had no pencil. My study hall teacher gave me permission to go to the library. I had a library slip from my study hall teacher that had to be signed by the librarian and returned.

The academic building was connected to the administration building, which housed the library, by an open walkway on the second-story level. As I crossed the walkway, a gust of wind tore my library slip from my hand. I grumbled to myself about the inconvenience of having to waste time and energy combating the gale in search of the lost slip of paper. Then quickly, I rationalized, "Why not use this as a time of praise?"

As I pondered the goodness and greatness of the Lord, a real God-given praise filled me, invigorating me. Soon I found my permission slip. It was lodged in the lower branches of a bush. Less than a foot from the bush lay the stub of a pencil! First, I was surprised. Then, realizing the gentle humor and faithful providence of the Lord, I threw back my head and laughed heartily. I felt He laughed with me.

When I was 15, it was a fad for schoolgirls to wear pennies in their loafers. I wore pennies in mine, but for a different purpose. It provided a protection for my conscience when I lied to my brother. Often he would ask me if I had any money. I would always say yes, usually referring to the two pennies in my shoes. It was incredible with what ingenuity I constructed a defense against asking or receiving legitimate help. My lack of trust surely wounded my good, generous brother. This indomitable independence caused me much unnecessary suffering. It would take years for me to overcome it even partially.

Before leaving B.T.S., I applied for employment for room and board for the following year. Surprise and disappointment nearly overwhelmed me when I was not employed, especially when a new student, and not a more eligible old student, got the job I was seeking. That kind of experience was all too common in life, so it was not too early to learn to cope with it positively.

The first step was to seek God's illumination about it. Being much too human, my emotions and intellect created so much static that I could not hear God until after many efforts to pray. Finally, He assured me there is no satisfying rational or emotional explanation for every human act. If I would relinquish the incident and trust Him, He had a plan for utilizing it for my spiritual growth and subsequent happiness. I promised to relinquish everything in perfect trust. Between the promised relinquishment and the perfected trust lies a great gap. But God lovingly, if not always gently, occupies in timely fashion every territory we surrender to Him.

It took a full year for me really to release the hurt I experienced by not being employed. But God kept His promise. The following year revealed a further broadening, of me as I advanced towards God's reality. Those horizons included learning to love and accept my own family in spite of their incomprehensible behavior.

Chapter 6

ONWARD IN FAITH

Beware of being hospitable to hurt. Harboring hurt created a gap in my wall of defense. Temptation wasted no time storming the gap. Hideous sins resulted when I was overcome by temptation. Subsequently, I lost my joy and peace. It all happened gradually.

The challenges I faced during one year at B.T.S. bore no resemblance to the expectations of my folks back home. Proud of their evaluation, I carefully concealed my inadequacies and strove to rise to their expectations, leading a double life - the real me, which I kept concealed, and the public me, whose maintenance absorbed all my mental and physical resources.

Upon arriving home, my primary desire was to find Ollie. She had been married a year and was living in Anniston, but she would not disclose her address. I knew she was expecting a baby. I had already prepared a place for her child in my heart, and I longed to share the last weeks of planning and waiting with her. I went to the Southern Bell Telephone Company where Ollie worked. I asked the supervisor for her address. She told me the name of the long avenue where Ollie lived, but she had no further information.

Undaunted, I started at the very beginning of the avenue. At every house or apartment I asked if Ollie lived there. Near the end of the avenue I found her. Triumphant joy filled me as I knocked on her door. I expected her to be pleased that I had found her.

Her husband opened the door. Seeing me from where she was sitting in the room, Ollie cried out, "What are you doing here? Go away and leave me alone. I want nothing to do with you."

Defying my shock, I entered her apartment. "Ollie," I said, "I wanted to see you. I love you, and I want to help you when the baby comes."

"I don't want your help," she replied. "Just go practice your religion elsewhere and leave me alone."

She refused to tell me when the baby was due. Further conversation with her was futile. Finally, I left her apartment baffled by her attitude.

Rushing to the church, I found a Sunday school room in the basement where I prayed. "Oh, God," I cried. "What have I done to Ollie that she hates me so? What can I do for her?"

It took me an hour to pray through sinful self-pity before I could hear the voice of God. "Act in response to the love you feel for her and ignore her behavior," He said.

Then, I had an idea. I would watch the newspapers every day until I saw the birth announcement. Then, I would go back to Ollie's house and help her.

In the meantime, our pastor invited me to go with his family to the Grand Canyon. He said I would be good company for his daughter on the trip, and they would pay all my expenses. What an opportunity! Or was it a temptation? Secretly, I hoped that my father would not permit me to go so I would be spared making the decision. I wanted desperately to go, but I knew if I were to "act in response to my love for Ollie" I could not go and forsake her when she would need my help. To make the temptation stronger my father told our pastor that I could go. The hard decision was mine to make. My sense of duty triumphed over my longings. I decided not to go.

While I watched the newspaper daily for the birth announcements, I participated in every phase of the church program. During this time I was strongly attracted to Mrs. Mae Jones, a beautiful Christian who had transferred her church membership to Anniston from Talladega. Her physical beauty, soft voice, prayers and testimonies, seasoned with extraordinary wisdom, won my heart. I was flattered when she invited me to join her and her husband in a street meeting ministry.

Mae Jones was prominent in the nucleus of "prayer warriors" in the church. When a special need arose, the prayer warriors would meet at the church and "pray through" about the problem. Inevitably, I joined these ladies in their prayer ministry, and more and more I became attached to Mae Jones.

Mae's wise instructions revealed her keen spiritual insight. We had regular one-sided Bible studies - one-sided because I would never advance an opinion or enter the discussion except to ask a question. Poor Mae wondered why I was so noncommittal. I refused to reveal to her that I was consciously, desperately trying to keep my ignorance concealed because every time I opened my mouth to speak, I revealed what I did not know. I became adept at keeping quiet. When cornered, I would escape by saying, "I don't know." Amazingly, she endured this enigma and continued to teach me. I had never met anyone who looked at my cocoon, so to speak, and saw a butterfly in the making. Her confidence in me was destined to become one of the most positive influences in my life.

On July 8, the newspaper announced that Mrs. McNaron had given birth to a boy the day before. Immediately, I went to see Ollie and baby Curtis. Joyfully, I washed clothes, cooked and cleaned. I loved the tiny baby boy and longed to cuddle him. Ollie, however, refused to allow me to touch the baby. Daily she would curse me and tell me not to come back again. Every day when I left her house I would go to the church to pray for understanding. After five days, Mama Floyd persuaded me not to go back. She said it was "casting my pearls before swine." My better judgment warned that I should go back, but I was not strong enough to heed it. Ollie never forgot that I had "forsaken her when Curtis was born."

B.T.S. moved to Cleveland in the summer of 1947. The name was changed to Lee College (now Lee University). My father said I could return to Lee College, but I would be responsible for all my expenses. Bitterly, I remembered that I did not get the job at school, so I could not pay my bill alone. I was resigned to staying in Anniston and attending school there.

Living at home was almost unbearable. I was 15 years old and still not supporting myself. I applied for a job as salesgirl in a dime store. They would not hire me even part-time until I could prove I was 16. By baby-sitting I earned enough to pay for my personal needs, but that did not relieve my fear that my father was weary of waiting for me to "stand on my own two feet." I compensated by doing my best schoolwork and being the best Christian I knew how to be. My father became extremely pensive. Since we had never established good communications, I could not imagine the cause of his loss of enthusiasm. Consequently, I felt like I was to blame.

Mama Floyd's attitude confirmed that fear. Often, she would tell me what she and my father would be free to do when I married or finished school. She told of trips they would take and clothes she planned to buy when my father no longer had the expense of supporting me. I withdrew more and more, making the situation worse. From the time school was out in the evenings until I left for school the next morning, I thought I would explode from the tensions of our home. My habit of going to the church to pray every day after school sustained me.

One day I lost myself in prayer, and the hours passed without my realizing it. It was getting dark when I arrived at home. My father and Mama Floyd were eating supper.

"Where have you been?" he asked.

"I went straight from the school to the church to pray," I replied.

"Oh, I don't doubt that! You probably met a car load of boys and there's no telling where you've been all this time," he accused.

For a moment I froze in startled silence. This was the same way Ollie had been falsely accused over and over until she revolted. Finally, I answered, "Nothing I can say will change your opinion. But if God lets me live long enough, my life-style will prove to you that your suspicions are erroneous." With that I retired to my room and resolved to find ways to stay away from the house as much as possible.

Mae Jones and I began to sing a duet. Nearly every afternoon I would go to her house. We would study the Bible, practice singing and pray. Mae worked in the mill, and her salary was small; but the biscuits, gravy, and fried salt pork at Mae's house tasted better than all the variety of foods on my father's table. I felt love and accepted as a daughter. I never once thought that I was an imposition.

Periodically, Ollie would call me to come and take care of Curtis while she worked. Her husband had left her, and the meager salary did not suffice for rent, groceries, and a baby-sitter. When her baby-sitter could not work, Ollie called me. She could not miss a day of work. How difficult it must have been for her to call me. I never refused, nor did I delay. Dropping everything, I literally ran the mile to her house so she would not be late for work.

Ollie never wanted me to do anything but keep Curtis. She kept her house spotlessly clean and her laundry washed and ironed. Her house was bare, and she never had any food, except for a few cans. Usually there was barely enough milk for the baby.

Since my father distrusted me for no reason, I understood why Ollie married. I pondered how dark and unpromising the future must have looked to her. At 17, sick and lonely, she had to struggle to rear her beloved baby with no light on her horizon to guide her. No one cared for her. My heart broke for her. Helplessly, I hugged Curtis to myself as I rocked him, praying audibly, tearfully that God would always keep His hand on Curtis and that He would reveal His own love and care to Ollie. Every time Ollie returned from work, she would tell me to go away and never return again.

"How can Ollie be so mean," I thought. It would take two more years for me to comprehend that her lashing out was against life itself, and I served only as a representative of the object of her frustration. I opened my heart to self-pity. I brooded over my home life. I thought my father did not love me and was weary of me. When my stepmother tried to get me to marry, I thought she was trying to rid herself of me. I resented her. I was proud of my patience with Ollie. What a pathetic state! Through the gap of harbored hurt, pride, resentment and self-pity, three of the most hideous of all sins thrived in my heart. My joy and peace departed. To make matters worse, I struggled to conceal this sinful state and fought to maintain the semblance of a victorious Christian. How could I confess that my "humility" was actually pride? How could I realize that withdrawal from my father could not be counted as having respect for his privacy? How could I admit that my long hours of daily prayer were little more than wallowing in self-pity before God's throne of grace? I was taking undue advantage of my right to His comfort. How could I divulge my resentments? By all means I had to keep up my pretense of holiness. But the burden of leading the double life was crushing me.

One evening, I was sitting pensively at Mae's house. She could tell something was wrong, so she asked me about it.

As long as we kept busy with impersonal matters, I was happy with Mae. But with this personal question I broke into uncontrollable tears. For an hour I cried and could not articulate a reason for it. Mae said, "You have to trust me enough to tell me what is troubling you or either you'll have to go home."

Determined to divulge the least possible, I blurted out, "I am so unhappy at home. My father doesn't love me."

Mae pressed me to explain myself. It is amazing how foolish and inadequate complaints sound when they are voiced. They are much more convincing when they silently torment the mind. Tolerantly, she listened to me. Then she asked me, "When did you last tell your father you loved him?"

"Me! Should I tell my father I love him? I'm too old to tell my father I love him," I exclaimed. "I show him my love by my excellent grades and my good conduct," I added. "And he shows you his love by his work and by caring for you," she insisted. "You are just like him. You want him to know you love him by your good works. Now I advise you, do not go to the church and pray your burden away. Go straight home and tell your father how much you love him and appreciate him," she instructed.

Seeing the wisdom in what she said, I resolved to try. All the way home I planned how I could tell my father I loved him. Suddenly, I recalled the time in Sylacauga when he did not give me away. His years of struggle and loneliness flashed before me. How could I have forgotten?

My father was sitting alone eating when I arrived home. Awkwardly, I tried to begin a conversation with him. He sensed my unnatural behavior and asked me about it.

"Oh, I have just been looking at myself, and I want to tell you what I saw," I explained.

"I have to go to the campground at Piedmont right now. You'll have to talk later," he said.

"Can I go with you?" I asked, thinking that in the dark car it would be easier to talk to him.

"Yes, if you get ready quickly, you can go, but we cannot be late," he replied.

Mama Floyd was at the camp meeting, and my father was going to bring her home. I washed the dishes while my father shaved and dressed. We were ready to go at the same time. To my dismay, my father picked up a couple who wanted to go to the camp meeting. I could not have a personal conversation with him in front of them.

When we arrived at the campground, the couple went into the tabernacle. I begged: "Please, let me talk to you two minutes."

"Well, but not longer. You know I've always been against people sitting in cars outside the tabernacle during service," he replied.

"Oh, Papa!" I began. "For such a long time I've brooded in self-pity thinking you didn't love me. I tried to prove I loved you by my scholastic achievements and my good conduct. I did not notice that you proved your love to me by keeping me and working hard for me." Throwing my arms around his neck I said, "I know you are the best father on earth, and I love you with all my heart."

My poor father wept. For a moment he could not speak. Finally, he said, "Yes, I do love my baby girl. When you were small, all you children climbed on me and told me you loved me. Since you've been grown, you are the only one who has ever told me."

My! How wise Mae had been! How I blessed her for pressing me to do something about my burden other than weeping it away in an hour of self-pity which I labeled "prayer."

I applied to Lee College for admission to the 1948-49 term of school and for a work scholarship. To my delight, it was granted. Already I was beginning to see how instructive my year in Anniston had been. Seeing in it God's plan, I relinquished my resentment for not having been employed the previous year. With that gap sealed, I could advance to the next step in God's plan.

Chapter 7

By Faith Into Rest

Lee College campus seemed like home to me. Stately Old Main surrounded by mature trees offered a warm reception. I loved its winding halls and quaint rooms. What a history this charming old building must have had. Enclosed in its protective walls, I received comfort.

My job was to clean the dormitory. With a thankful heart I resolved to do my work as unto the Lord. Diligently, I went about cleaning as if the Master Himself would pass by and use the facilities I had prepared. The idea of working for Jesus sparked worshipful praise in my heart, and I sang while I worked. Those who heard me were not always pleased.

Although I was liberated from the tension of my home, my search for spiritual reality continued to preoccupy me. Too many inconsistencies existed in my life. My apparently beautiful Christian character was only superficial. The strain of trying to maintain it exhausted me. Compliments often paid to my humility or my sincerity insulted and condemned me. I knew no way out of my problem except through more legalism. I fasted more and prayed more, not realizing that my spiritual problem was legalism. For all my striving, my situation did not change. Exhausted, I sought for a counselor but found no one who could help me. Like Paul I cried out, "O wretched man that I am! Who shall deliver me from the body of this death?" (Romans 7:24).

One night in early winter I could not sleep. My spiritual dilemma oppressed me. My thoughts turned to my father. From all I had observed, he seemed to have experienced spiritual reality. He was not striving like me. He was resting, or at least so it seemed. How does one enter rest and cease from striving, I wondered?

Finally, I got up from my bed, took a pencil and paper and went to the restroom where I could use the lights after curfew. I wrote the following poem:

To Dad

I love you, Dad

Because you taught me how to live

To learn, to play and to give.

You taught me how to love

The beauties of earth

As well as things above.

Full many a day I sat upon your knee

And joyfully learned the songs

you sang to me.

Your eyes would sparkle with a holy light

As we would gather around the fire at night

A Special Note...

Auburn — 21
Ala. 22

To worship God who kept us day by day.

Everyone in his own simple way

Would lift his voice in earnest fervent prayer.

The sacredness of that devotion

Was felt as it would penetrate the air.

Do these sweet memories have to flee from me?

May I not cherish yet their company?

If not, then make me now a child,

Let me be back again a little while.

Life is not sugar plums, sweetmeats and creams.

It is as a violent, rushing stream

Running swiftly down to the river wide,

Beating furiously its banks on either side.

Thanks to the Maker and your faith so true

I know life's problems, whether great or few

Can be surrendered to the One who cares.

Hope and peace can then replace despair.

I love you, Dad,

For these things you have taught,

For knowledge of life's battles you have fought.

Oh, that I the secret now may learn

To meet face to face with all concern

The battle, and fight as I never fought before.

You won those conflicts, those bitter wars.

I can win and I must never lose

There are but two paths from which to choose:

The path of victory or the path of defeat,

Which no one really is compelled to meet.

When we at last have had our final test

And proved to all that we have done our best,

It matters not which path it appeared to be.

One's best travels only the path of victory.

The formula was there: "I know life's problems whether great or few can be surrendered to the One who cares. Hope and peace then can replace despair." However, knowing how to surrender was so veiled in legalism that it would take two more years before I learned to work out the formula and find rest.

Margareta Poulos was again my dormitory supervisor. She was very pleased with my work. Knowing that I was solely responsible for my expenses, she would recommend me to city people who wanted to hire students for odd jobs.

Margareta was not sentimental, but she was fair. She strove to encourage anyone who was trying. Like Mae Jones, Margareta recognized something valid in me. Her confidence in me gave me incentive and turned my work into a joy instead of a chore.

All I could earn I paid immediately on my bill. Often I could not afford personal items that I needed. Once when I was caught in this predicament, Beatrice Coley called me to her room.

"Margaret," she said, "anytime you need anything just go to the store and buy it and charge it to my account. You don't need to tell me or anyone else."

This proposition amazed me. What trust! Who was I that my English Literature teacher would place such confidence in me? Never did I use that privilege, but I constantly drew courage and inspiration from that trust. I thought, "To be trusted is to be saved."

I was unusually blessed. Three people really trusted me. It was not the hopeful uneasy trust of an anxious parent; it was the confident assurance of a friend. Mae Jones was first to trust me. Then, Margareta and Bea trusted me. Their trust inspired me to trust myself. If they could look upon my imperfections as an unsightly cocoon and believe inside was concealed a butterfly, why should I not also believe that I was more than a worm. Encouraged by a new self-vision I was spurred on to the highest goals.

Being a perfectionist, I applied myself totally to everything I undertook to do. My mind's tireless thrust taxed my physical capabilities. I was driven to excel scholastically. In spite of my incredible workload, I enjoyed numerous extra-curricular activities. My secret spiritual dilemma constrained me to fast days and often weeks at a time and spend long hours in prayer. Physically, I buckled under the strain. Anemia slowed me down. Mentally, I was harassed mostly because of my slow spiritual progress. No one knew how nearly overwhelmed I was. Faith and hope sustained me.

Nearing the end of the school term as a senior in high school, I was nominated to receive the Danforth Leadership Award. The committee in charge of determining honorees had a controversy as to whether or not I should receive it. Since I was salutatorian of my class, a member of the Beta Club, and one of the five Who's Who of my class, they proposed giving the Danforth Leadership Award to someone else. Here Bea Coley and Margareta opposed the suggestion. An honor must be earned, not simply shared, they said. To their satisfaction I had duly earned the honor, and it was only fair that I receive it regardless of whether or not I had earned every honor in the institution. They prevailed, and I received the

Danforth Leadership Award. Again, it was the confidence, rather than the award itself, which was so meaningful to me. I pledged to live up to the confidence that had been invested in me. I committed myself to justifying that trust.

At age 17, graduating from high school was my first big achievement. My excitement joined with that of my classmates. They shared theirs with family and friends. I shared mine with Mae Jones who was the sole visitor at my graduation. I had hoped that my father would come, as I considered any honor I had earned was his own and his name that I bore would be honored. My father did not share that philosophy. He assured me that he believed each one is responsible to make or break his or her own reputation.

The summer of 1949 passed quickly. I stayed with Ada and took care of her children while she worked. I did not have to return to my father's house. Although I enjoyed keeping house for my sister, I was happier still to return to Lee College in the fall. As salutatorian of my class I received a $200 scholarship. It was too little to help but too much to relinquish. The scholarship with my employment for my room and board was incentive enough to drive me on.

The 1949-50 school term, possibly the greatest in the history of Lee College, began enthusiastically. The energetic student body outpaced the faculty's abilities to plan meaningful activities. Consequently, the students proceeded to organize clubs to their own liking. Not least among them was the Dirty Dozen. Made up of twelve of the most intelligent and enterprising young men in college, this club spelled frustration for the administration. The Dirty Dozen's gusto for mischief manifested itself in most ingenious pranks. The students relished both the mischief of the pranksters and the frustration of the faculty.

Having little reprieve from my work, I had no social

life at Lee. Friendly with everyone, I nevertheless had no close friends. Dr. David J. DePlessis's daughter was an exception. Newly arrived in our country from South Africa, she was unfamiliar with our customs and rarely left her home. Frequently, I visited her and richly benefited from my acceptance in her well-governed family. I absorbed Mrs. DuPlessis's warm, motherly manner. The evident mutual trust and respect among family members relaxed me. The gentle but firm discipline of Dr. DuPlessis established the family security. Even now I experience deep satisfaction as I remember that ideal home.

During the winter the administration at Lee College came under extreme pressures. The college was in great financial debt and could not cope with new expenses. The spiritual debt was even greater as many of the students left God. Their mischief was taking its toll on the nerves of the faculty. President Stewart Brinsfield's facial expression and the stoop of his shoulders betrayed the invisible weight that pressed upon him. As the situation grew steadily worse, some of the students began to pray for revival. No doubt the faculty had already been praying. A spring revival was scheduled, but the survival of the college demanded hasty divine intervention.

That intervention arrived on a Sunday in February. During what was expected to be just another chapel service, the power of God rushed through the auditorium. Every individual was shaken by the overwhelming power. Students were saved and healed. Even students lying sick in the dormitories experienced a sudden rush of healing power and came to the auditorium to testify. The Spirit gripped the student body so forcefully that no one wanted to leave the auditorium. For three days and nights meals were forgotten, classes were dismissed, and we slept very little. Even some strangers passing the campus in their automobiles were seized by the mighty power and stopped to inquire what was going on.

In the auditorium students spontaneously brought offerings for the college. Those who did not have money gave their watches, their cars, or their free labor. Thus, the debts were paid and the expenses could be met. Possibly every student and faculty member had a new birth, a frank renewal during that spontaneous, heaven-sent revival. Most, if not all, of the Dirty Dozen were converted and called to the ministry. Some of the most outstanding ministers in the Church of God today were previous organizers of the Dirty Dozen.

After the high tides of power subsided, the afterglow of the revival hovered over the school for the remainder of the year. I venture to say that the glow of that revival has never completely vanished from those who were there and participated in it.

About the time of the revival I began to date Curtis Stokes. I talked about my call to North Africa. He told me that he had been in the North African campaign during the World War II. He described how he had been a sinner then and he would like to return as a Christian to proclaim the salvation message. The friendship seemed naturally to be leading to love and marriage, but as our discussions became more intimate, fear gripped me. I recalled my mother's lifelong conflict trying to harmonize her mission call and housewife responsibilities. How could I do better than my mother? How could I give my heart to a man when I had given it irrevocably to God and to missions? Since Curtis did not have a definite mission call, I could not expect him to go to North Africa. Abruptly, I discontinued all contact with Curtis. Burying myself in my work, I retrieved my heart before it was lost irreparably.

In an effort to cut expenses, I stayed in summer school in 1950, and I took extra jobs to pay my bill. It never once occurred to me that anyone could leave school owing a debt. The responsibility was mine, and I determined to pay what I owed.

When school opened in September, I realized that I would soon finish Lee College. I would have to make some decision about what I would do next. It was certainly a major step in my life and deserved my seeking God's guidance.

During this time I received a letter from Miss Josephine Planter. Several times over the past six years I had corresponded with her, but I was surprised to get her letter. She pleaded with me to come help her. She was already past 80 years old and alone. Who would take over her work? I heard her appeal in my deepest soul and thought it was the next step I should take. I decided to take the letter to the Executive Missions Secretary and volunteer to go.

The Rev. J.H. Walker Sr., who was Executive Missions Secretary at the time, said, "The Board members are presently deliberating about whom to send to Tunisia. This letter certainly comes at an opportune time, however, I do not think the Board would expect God to answer in this way. Nevertheless, would you like to meet the Board?"

"Yes, I shall be pleased to meet them," I agreed.

In the fall of 1950 I met the World Missions Board for the first time.

I was still only 18 years old. When I walked into the presence of those gentlemen, their formidable combined dignity struck me dumb. All my vulnerability clothed me. How could this timid, single 18-year old possibly be God's choice for a missionary to Tunisia? The Missions Board rejected my request to be sent. The devastating message came soon after my nineteenth birthday.

This great disappointment plunged me into an overpowering darkness of despair. The despair was not produced solely by the rejection of the Missions Board. Another factor was my total exhaustion from years of overwork. The most crucial factor, however, was the spiritual crisis within me that had been building up for a long time: my sense of shame or lack of spiritual reality.

I felt like such a fraud. I felt that everyone had been praising me for being such a great Christian, while underneath I saw the terrible imperfections of it, the non-reality of it. I had sought relief by talking to some of the more spiritual students and faculty members and several mentors. All I had received were blank stares and total incomprehension. They said the same thing: "Margaret, you're an exemplary Christian. We wish everyone were like you."

I did not feel complimented by such words but only more frustrated, for they left me with no help for the emptiness I knew was inside me. I thought, "If these are the best mentors I know, and they can't see through me any better than that and they don't understand the fraud, the lack of reality, then to whom shall I go?"

Miss Planter was begging me to come. I had gotten her letter in answer to praying and fasting and waiting on the Lord for what I should do when I finished Lee College. "Surely, this is the next step!" I had thought. "Surely, the World Missions Board will see it this way. Surely, they will see the connection between my fervent prayer to God and Miss Planter's fervent letter of invitation to me!"

I was totally unprepared for the rejection, or what I took as the rejection of the Missions Board. Of course, now it is easy to understand why they did not see it my way. After all, I was only 18 years old at the time. It was a serious matter to send an 18-year-old single girl to the far-off land of Tunisia to be with an 85-year-old woman who could suddenly die at any time. I am sure they were seeing many possibilities and eventualities for which they were not prepared to take responsibility. Nevertheless, their rejection, coming as it did on top of my long struggle with feeling like a fraud, struck me like a final, confirming blow.

After a few days' initial struggle with the despair, I made the startling discovery that I really did not believe anything anymore. With the Board's decision reinforcing my prior recognition of being a fraud, the whole business of God struck me as just much ado about nothing! "It's all unreal. It's a show. It doesn't work," I said to myself.

Nevertheless, I had no alternative. I was lonely. The whole God quest had come to nothing, and yet I had nothing else. It was my only tether to life.

I did not feel free to go back to my family. If finishing high school carried with it the expectation "to stand on your own two feet," get a job and take care of yourself, then how much more would that be true of finishing college? I did not feel free to go back home, and I did not have hope of going to the mission field. My whole life was such an unreal fraud. Just a fraud! No one could understand, and no one could advise me.

Although this state of despair lasted only a matter of days (not weeks, months, or years, thank God!), it was nonetheless an unbearable dark, dark hopelessness—a blackness. From time to time it seemed as if I would come up for air, and I would see a little glimpse of blue between these dark clouds. Something in me would cry out, "O God, keep me; I can't keep myself!" Then clouds would cover things. The blue would be gone, and I would be plunged back into the darkness. It was an awful place—a lonely, lost, hopeless place where you do not have any people and you do not have any God. I was alone on a deserted campus through the duration of the Christmas break.

When the darkness cleared a little, I took my Bible and I ran to the prayer room. I spread my Bible out before the Lord, and I said: "I don't understand you or your Bible, God. Here you say, 'every tree therefore which bringeth not forth good fruit is hewn down, and cast into the fire' (Luke 3:9).

"I know and I'm not ashamed to tell you, because you know it's true, that from the time I gave you my heart until now I have done my dead-level best to be a good Christian. From the time you called me to the mission field until now I've done my best to be prepared to fulfill that call. I see that I'm not real. I'm such a fraud! If you want fruit, I don't have even one scrawny, wormy green apple that I can offer you. Furthermore, God, I don't promise you that I'll ever have any fruit, because I've done my dead-level best—and you can't do better than your best—and my best has failed. All I know how to do now is just to wait here at your altar, because I don't have anywhere else to go."

I waited for what seemed to me a long time. It was cold in that prayer room. Students had not yet come back to the dormitory from holiday break, and the heat had not been turned back on. It was a cold day in January 1951 in Nora Chambers Hall. People were celebrating the New Year, and there I sat in my darkness—limp. I had said everything I knew to say and cried everything I knew to cry.

Finally, a calm voice broke the silence. "I didn't ask you to bear fruit."

I said, "You what? You didn't ask me to bear fruit? What does this mean: 'the tree therefore which bringeth not forth good fruit is hewn down, and cast into the fire'?"

He said, "That didn't ask you to bear fruit. I have been waiting all this time for you to quit trying so hard and just do what you said you are going to do now—just abide on my altar. For my word says: 'If ye abide in me, and my words abide in you, ye shall bring forth much fruit.' But it won't be any effort on your part. You don't have to produce it. You will be *fruitful*. You will even be unaware of how much fruit you have. It will be there, but it won't be your efforts. Just abide in me, and let my word abide in you."

I felt so relieved—relieved from the burden of having to be a good Christian or having to be anything! All I had to be was His beloved child. That was such a grand privilege that suddenly I was flooded with joy, and I recognized *that* as a fruit! I had great peace, and I recognized *that* as a fruit! All of my resentments for all those happy, young people who did not try half as hard as I did melted away, because I now felt no envy for their place. I was loving them instead of resenting them, and I was longing for them to enter into this wonderful experience that was surely the best way to celebrate a new year. This love I had for them I recognized as a fruit!

Before I left that room, I realized that all kinds of fruits were on me. This was true not because I had decorated my tree. I had not tied those things on myself. They had been miraculously produced from inside by the Spirit. From that moment the Lord was free to begin to teach me. I was free to abide in His presence. This was my prerequisite and preparation for the next step—a step into the vastness.

Chapter 8

Out Into Vastness

*D*elivered from the tyranny of legalism, if not completely from the practice thereof, I rested in my freedom and infant faith. I no longer needed to be a double person. Guarding my simple reality became my ultimate objective. Pure joy filled my heart for the first time in my life. The energy economized from not having to maintain my shame empowered me for a new adventure. That new adventure with God began as I left Lee College in January 1951.

Refusing to accept the decision of the Missions Board as final, I made a plan. I transferred my college credits to a college nearer home. There I would work and continue my education until I got a degree.

The Southern Bell Telephone Company employed me and within two months gave me all their training. All was set for me to work and save some money for my tuition. The spring and summer passed with everything going according to plan.

On the first day of registration at college I fell suddenly ill and was hospitalized. I was not released from the hospital until after the final date of registration. Surprised, I resorted to prayer. "Lord," I prayed, "I applied to the World Missions Board and was rejected. Then I prepared to continue my education, but these plans have been thwarted. Now it is up to you to show me the next step I am to take."

Relinquishing the matter, I rested and waited.

Two weeks later, Mable Branch was speaking in the Sunday morning service in Anniston. For her text she read Psalm 37:4-5: "Delight thyself also in the Lord; and he shall give thee the desires of thine heart. Commit thy way unto the Lord; trust also in him; and he shall bring it to pass."

Usually, I listened intently to hear what God was telling me in a sermon. This time I was distracted by my own meditations. Hearing the text, I reasoned: "Here is a condition and a promise. Provided I meet the condition the promise is mine."

What was the condition? "Delight thyself in the Lord." Mentally reliving my life with poignant emotional detail, I concluded: "Lord, you are my unique delight. Whom have I on earth besides you and whom do I desire in heaven above you?" I realized I fulfilled the condition.

"The promise, then, is mine!" I affirmed. "…and he shall give thee the desires of thy heart."

"Now I have the desires of my heart. But what are the desires of my heart so I can praise God when I receive them?" I mused.

I could think of only two desires that I cherished. "Lord," I prayed, "You are the desire of nations. Realizing you to the fullest human capacity is my first desire. Also, I want to fulfill my call to the mission field in Tunisia. Any other desires are subservient to that."

Immediately Satan challenged me. "What you really desire is a big name and many admirers," he accused. This was only the first time he so accused me, but many times through the years he would instigate accusers to make the same accusation. This first time took me completely by surprise.

Knowing the deceitfulness of the human heart, I left my defense up to God and resumed my silent prayer: "Is it possible that my heart is so deceitful as to harbor such a motive? If so, Lord, send me to a place where I have no communication with anyone. Let me serve in a secluded, unknown spot."

With that prayer uttered, I mentally returned to the service and heard Sister Branch terminate her sermon with the words, "Fear not, you have the desires of your heart." Not realizing that I had mentally shut out Sister Branch's sermon by my meditations, I heard her closing statement as a distantly uttered prophesy which was peculiarly my own. My faith claimed it. My spirit rejoiced in it. My mind perceived it to imply that I would soon be leaving for Tunisia. Immediately, I felt as though an immense crystal ball descended and covered me. Inside was pure peace. Quietly I rejoiced with tears streaming down my cheeks.

"Margaret, what is wrong?" someone asked.

"Nothing is wrong," I answered. "Everything is perfectly right. I shall soon be leaving for Tunisia."

"How do you know?" came the reply. "Has the Missions Board reversed its decision?"

"I know nothing about the Missions Board," I stated. "I only know the triune board of heaven just approved it, and I'll certainly be going."

With obvious sarcasm the person asked, "How soon will you be going?"

The question caught me off guard. I had not pondered

my date of departure. An internal voice beyond my own intellect answered for me, "The exact date of departure isn't yet fixed, but before a year passes I shall be settled in Tunisia."

As I left the church, I was enraptured to realize that I could commit my way unto the Lord and trust in Him. He would bring it to pass.

I returned to the furnished apartment that I rented from one of the church members. The sister even furnished the linens, but I stored them and used my own. Acting on the new revelation, I packed my linens, and began to use those that were furnished. While I ironed my linens to pack them, the following poem came as my prayer.

My Choice

'Tis not an easy path that I would choose

A shady lane or rosy lined way.

'Tis not a knowledge great that I desire

To comprehend the steps I take each day.

'Tis not an easy burden I long to bear

A cross that's light or one that's bright and gay

But 'tis to tell my heart so, Master, dear,

That Thou art there to lead Thy child always.

I would not choose a swirl of glowing fame

A world-known name, a man-called victory

Nor would I choose a place of great renown

Or a statue of honor erected unto me.

I would not long to shun life's aches and pains
Or man's harsh words or hasty judgments flee
For Thou alone art Judge so who can blame
When 'tis Thy heart alone I seek to please.

First I long to know that Thou art near
Second that Thou doest understand and care
Third to hear Thee speak my soul to cheer
And to lift above all doubt, gloom and despair
Fourth to be found working night and day
To fulfill the commission Thou has given
Finally, to see You face to face some day
And be received into Your blissful heaven.

After I recorded this poem and packed my trunk, I waited.

The wait was long. From October to February God spoke not a word. Those at church who had heard my testimony rejected it as pure imagination and forgot it. Never once did I doubt. My trunk stayed packed while I waited for God's next instructions.

In February 1952, I had four consecutive days off. Since this was a new experience, I prayed about it: "Lord, do you have a purpose of your own for giving me four days? Do you have something you want me to do?"

"Go to Birmingham and apply for your passport and book your passage to Tunisia," came the silent but undeniable reply.

Even I was surprised. Although I knew I would receive God's guidance, the time, place and manner of His revelation astonished me. Thrilled that I was to make definite travel plans, I forgot all the implications entirely.

On Thursday, Mrs. Williams, a devout Baptist and sister to a member of our church, called me and asked, "What are you planning to do tomorrow?"

"I'm going to Birmingham," I replied with the ease of one who knew Birmingham like the back of her hand.

"Are you going shopping?" she asked.

"No, I'm going to apply for my passport and book my passage to Tunisia," I answered.

"What! I thought you had forgotten about going to Tunisia," she exclaimed.

"No, never," I affirmed. "I was only quietly waiting for God's time."

"Then I'm going to take you to Birmingham in the car," she stated.

"Fine. I'll give you my bus fare for gasoline," I proposed.

"No, if you are going to the mission field, I want to be the first one to contribute to your support," she said.

To hear me speak, one would have thought I was well informed. In reality, I had no idea where to go to apply for a passport or where to go to book passage on a steamship. With $10.25 in my pocket, I planned to pay my roundtrip fare on the Greyhound Bus, apply for a passport and book passage on a steamship halfway around the world.

Fortunately, Mrs. Williams was better informed. She took me straight to the courthouse where I applied for my passport. When asked who was going to sign my application with me to witness my good conduct record, Mrs.

Williams quickly stated that she had come for that purpose. I gave the clerk one dollar. Then I went downstairs to the post office and made a money order for nine dollars to the State Department for the passport. That left me 25 cents.

After we had eaten at a restaurant, Mrs. Williams took me to the Brownell Travel Bureau. I wondered whether she knew that I had never so much as heard of a travel bureau before. I wondered whether she comprehended that she was divinely sent to be my guide and advisor.

Entering the travel bureau, I responded intelligently as though I had frequently traveled. When asked what I wanted, I replied: "I want to book passage to Tunisia."

"Which port do you plan to go to?" asked the clerk.

"Tunis," I answered, not knowing there was any other port in Tunisia.

"When do you plan to embark?"

"As soon as possible," I answered. "Do you have a schedule of departure dates from which I could choose?"

The clerk showed me the dates of embarkation and the plan of the ship. I chose April 2 as my tentative departure date and a stateroom on the steamship *Constitution.*

"When and how am I expected to pay the fare?" I asked, holding my breath for fear she would request some money down.

"You pay nothing until you receive the confirmation of your reservation," she informed me to my tremendous relief. "You must pay the total fare within one month of departure. You may write a check to this office," she explained.

"That is fine," I said. The fact that I had less than three weeks in which to pay my total fare did not disturb me.

"Where have you been?" I was asked when I returned to Anniston and to church.

"I was in Birmingham for my passport and my ticket to Tunisia," I answered.

"Haven't you heard the news? War broke out in Tunisia. No one can enter or leave. You can't go," came the reply.

"No, I haven't heard the news nor am I informed of current events in Tunisia. Nevertheless, my communications with a higher authority are clear. He knows the current events and it is He who guided me. He will work out His plan with perfect timing," I declared.

The church was perplexed about its role. If God were really leading me, they wanted to help me. If I were deceived, they wanted to hinder me. How could they know? Finally, the council agreed that if God allowed me to complete all my travel plans with no hindrance, they would help me. Within two weeks I received my confirmation of passage as well as my passport. My feet scarcely touched the ground. My joy was complete.

The Internal Revenue Service reimbursed me $74. Fifty-four dollars, which I had saved for tuition to college, and many unexpected offerings handed to me personally sufficed to pay my passage to Tunisia. The church gave me an offering and the Pentecostal Holiness Church invited me to speak and gave me an offering. By the time of my departure, my fare, my suitcases and clothes were bought, and I had $100 over all that expense. What a miracle it was to me! How happy I was when I held my fully paid ticket in my hand!

About noon, on March 25, 1952, I boarded the Southern train in Anniston on my way to New York. My father and stepmother and several friends saw me off at the station. The quiet parting was in no way indicative of the adventures that lay ahead.

On April 2, I boarded the S.S. *Constitution*. Pre-occupied with all the activities and fanfare of the departing steamship, I ignored that there was no one to see me off. From a diary I kept at the time I'll quote my memoirs of the actual embarkation.

"'All ashore who is going ashore,' came the cry. The band began to play, *Should Old Acquaintance Be Forgotten*. Everyone waved their goodbye, while ticker tape and confetti filled the air. Finally the band played *Anchors Aweigh*, and the steamship's horn blasted a long, melancholy signal of departure. All was quiet and still. Everyone waved while only an occasional sob and the lapping of the waves against the ship broke the silence. Did I wave? Of course, I waved to America. As I waved I prayed, "God, keep her free."'"

On April 16, at 9 o'clock in the morning, I arrived in Tunisia. Miss Planter and some of her friends met me at the port. Miss Planter had a bouquet of flowers, a big smile and wide-open arms for me. Immediately, I loved her, and I loved my adopted land.

Arriving at Miss Planter's house, the welcoming party had a thanksgiving prayer for my safe arrival. Then Miss Planter, sure that I was totally exhausted from my long trip, insisted that I go to bed for a rest. Actually, I was too curious about my new land and my new home to want to sleep, but it was easier to comply than to explain.

The bed was a thin straw mattress on a cot springs next to Miss Planter's bed. A handkerchief with "Margaret" embroidered on it in royal blue was folded in a triangle and placed on the pillow. Lying on the handkerchief was a bouquet of crocheted pink bells. I could imagine with what kind, even tender, thought they were put there.

While I rested, Miss Planter boiled a whole chicken with some vegetables. It was meant to strengthen me after my trip and she expected me to eat it all, including the head, feet and the tripe. The custom of cleaning the head and tripe and cooking them with the chicken was too new for me to appreciate.

Miss Planter doted on me with all her pent-up motherly instinct. She planned for me to inherit everything she possessed. She wanted me to learn French, Arabic and Hebrew. All the rich promises she received from God she expected to be mine as her own promised child and heir. From today's vantage point, I can see that she would have spared nothing to bring her plan to pass. I was under no pressure to do anything except study and prepare myself for my full inheritance.

Three very real hindrances totally blocked that desirable plan. I was too impulsive; I was too independent; and the three-generation gap between my 20 years and her 85 years made mutual comprehension and communication impossible. What an opportunity I had to relax and study for three years before Miss Planter died, and at the same time make that poor weary missionary's last years happy and restful.

But I was too impulsive. I had already spent six years in preparation after receiving my mission call. God had led me so miraculously. Surely, He did not intend for me to be shut in a dark apartment gorging myself on languages while the teeming multitudes passing under my balcony totally ignored the salvation plan. There simply had to be some way I could serve even while I studied. I ignored the marvelously relaxed pace of our Lord.

In three months I began conversing in French. At least, I could understand French well enough to be a good listener. At that time Miss Planter had some elderly friends in the hospital and she allowed me to go visit them without a chaperone. Thus began a hospital ministry that lasted until I left Tunis.

Notice I said she "allowed" me to visit the hospital. This brings me to the second hindrance. I was too independent.

What a cataclysmic adjustment! All my life I had been

trained to stand on my own two feet. Four years I had actually achieved that goal. Now I was suddenly forced to depend on Miss Planter for instruction, for protection and for support. I secretly rebelled at asking her permission to go anywhere, even with a chaperone. She expected me to accept her plan for my future with no resistance. She wanted me to depend upon her financially without discussing the slightest need with me. Everything in me stood firm in silent rebellion. All my energy was wasted in trying to figure out why she was so obstinate and how I could escape from her without disrespecting her.

Finally, there was the gap of at least three generations between us. In Bohemia, the land of her birth, adulthood began at 30. At 20 I still had 10 years of adolescence left! I steadfastly resisted such a concept.

"My own father trusted me to come all the way to Tunisia alone," I said to her one day. "Why can't you trust me to go one block to the market alone?"

Had the truth been told, my father did not trust me. In fear and trembling he tried to trust God to keep me. He knew of the vice in the world. He knew my naivete. He would have appreciated the security that Miss Planter's overprotectiveness gave me.

No doubt Miss Planter grieved when I silently rejected her wholesome plan. When I persistently struggled to escape, she probably saw me as being most ungrateful. Every time I prayed for deliverance, the Lord told me, "You don't have the right attitude. So long as you cannot leave with love and peace dominating your heart, you must stay here."

Some days Miss Planter would sit down and tell me stories of her beloved natal land. Her face transfigured as she proceeded from childhood pranks to adolescent love to her call to God's service, concluding with the crescendo of worship with some beautiful hymn, which she sang surprisingly well. Enraptured by the beauty of her face and the magnetism of the moment, I loved her deeply. She had to be a saint.

One day she returned home after walking several miles in 120° heat. She had battled undisciplined crowds all morning to get a small package out of customs. The duties she finally paid were thrice the value of the package.

Entering the house, she threw the package across the room shouting: "Cursed be that package that tormented a tired, old missionary. Cursed be the person that sent it. Cursed be the customs official who overcharged for such a useless thing." Then shaking her fist at heaven she said, "If there were another God beside you, I'd go to Him and complain against You!'

Aghast at such behavior, I thought she would certainly fall dead for defying God! Even I could understand the kindness of the crippled girl who had sent the scuffs and a pair of men's wool socks. She lived on welfare and supported her aged mother and her sick brother. Her means were limited. She only hoped Miss Planter's weary feet could find rest in the scuffs and be kept warm by the wool socks in winter. Her intentions had to be beautiful. "Ungrateful old woman. How could she curse anyway?" I questioned. "She has to have a devil."

In fact, when I corresponded with Mae Jones, I alternately called Miss Planter a saint and a devil. I finally gave up trying to understand her and left the labeling to heaven. Since then my own experience has given me a great deal of understanding.

One morning I was praying alone after Miss Planter went to her Bible Depot, a shop where she displayed Bibles and gave lessons. A knock came at the door. Fear swept over me like an icy breeze, and the hair on my arms stood up. Not given to fear, I wondered what the strange premonition could mean. Opening the door, I saw a young man who had been to our door before.

"Good day," I greeted him.

"Good day," he answered. "Is your mother home?"

"No, she isn't," I answered, not realizing he was just wanting to find me at home alone. "You can find her at her Bible Depot today."

"Do you have any old newspapers to sell?" he asked.

"No, I'm sorry. We do not buy the newspaper," I answered, remembering he had asked me the same question on another occasion and received the same answer.

"Will you give me a drink of water before I go?" he asked, hoping I would leave the door open so he could get in.

"Yes, just wait," I replied, shutting the door and making sure the night-latch caught.

He drank one sip of the water. Throwing the glass of water in my eyes in order to confuse me, he thrust himself at the narrowly opened door. The premonition had not been wasted. With unnatural strength I slammed the door shut, catching his right arm which he wrenched painfully out of the crack.

Secure at last, I weakly staggered back to my place of prayer.

"Thank you, God, for the warning," I prayed. "Thank you, also, for giving me a peek at the totally unknown dangers that lurk in this mysterious land. Yes, Lord, thank you for this dreadful, intolerable protectiveness with which Miss Planter overshadows me. I knelt today to complain. You have turned my complaint to a blessing."

That episode greatly altered my attitude. Shortly thereafter, I was praying again. "Lord, I do not understand why I am here. You will not let me leave. Now I relinquish my striving. I'll stay here all my life or as long as Miss Planter lives if that is what you want. She has done and said so many things to destroy my reputation without my having the slightest possibility to defend myself. There is nothing left to salvage. I give up," I cried painfully.

Two weeks later, Miss Planter wrote me a note and placed it on my night table. "Margaret, You make my life a hell. Please, find yourself somewhere else to stay."

I welcomed the open door with no resentment. Real love and pity had replaced my antagonism. However, it would take years before I could understand the possibility of my best efforts creating "hell" for her.

If I had not been capable of receiving Miss Planter's plan, God had an alternate plan for me. From May 1953, I was alone with Him to discover His plan.

Chapter 9

Alone With God

Alone. The freedom for which I had struggled for months loomed gigantic before me. I was so conscious of being alone that I scarcely realized I was with God.

Where would I go? How and what would I teach? With the questions came the assurance that I was with God and He had the answers.

Stepping out of Miss Planter's house, I entered a fascinating world of formidable contrast. How painfully insignificant I was on the crowded streets. Roman gladiators, Barbarian pirates, Carthaginian merchants, Arabian conquerors, and even Saint Augustine had all preceded me in Tunisia. Each had left his influence. My vulnerability was surpassed only by the grace of God. To that grace I appealed for protection and guidance.

My command of the French language facilitated my

finding a new home. Frankly, I had not the slightest notion where to search. After seeking God for guidance, I got on a streetcar at random. An Italian lady who attended the Baptist church saw me. "Aren't you the American who lives with Miss Planter?" she asked.

"Yes I am. How do you know me?" I replied.

"I saw you once with Miss Planter at a fellowship meeting. Where are you going now?" she inquired.

"Miss Planter has asked me to move from her house, so I am looking for a room," I answered.

"Maybe I have the answer for you," she said. "My neighbor is a widow with three girls. She wants to rent a room to supplement her income. Do you think you would like to see her?"

"Yes, and I should be grateful to you to show me the way," I replied.

I rented a small bedroom with kitchen privileges in Megrine, about five miles from Tunis.

Because my belongings were so few, I was quickly settled in my new home. Losing no time, I began visiting from house to house to introduce myself and to witness for Christ. I explained frankly that the power of God transforms the hearts and lives of believers in Him. In each home I requested permission to teach children the Bible. The people received me graciously, and many children promised to come to the Bible class.

Events had developed very quickly. In an effort to concentrate only on God, I fasted three days, waiting before the Lord. "Oh, God," I prayed, "my hour has come and I am too ignorant. What would you have me do? I do not want to indoctrinate trusting children in anything that will bring them into bondage from which they will have to find deliverance in the future. I want to teach them what they should know. How will I know what to teach?"

"Simply teach them to love my Word and to trust my Spirit. Teach by precept and by example—this is all I require," He deeply impressed me.

One day I was in a neighboring village on a mission. Returning late in the afternoon, I realized it would be dark before I reached Megrine. "Father," I prayed, "it wasn't very wise of me to return so late. I was doing your work, however, so it is your business to see me safely home."

From the train station to my house was half a mile. The path led by a wheat field on the left and a quagmire on the right. Soon after I left the train, I heard footsteps behind me.

"I'll slacken my pace," I thought. "If that is someone going to my village, I'll let them pass me and I'll follow them closely for company. If it is someone who intends me harm," I reasoned, "I'll want to face it as soon as possible because I cannot escape."

When I slackened my pace, I could tell that the footsteps behind me quickened. Suddenly a strange man was standing to my left.

"Stop!" he commanded.

"You are a stranger to me," I said. "In case you intend me harm, I think it is only fair to warn you. I'm not alone as you suppose. The Father, Son and Holy Spirit are with me to defend me."

"Haw, Haw, Haw! She still believes in Santa Claus," he scornfully replied, stretching out his arms to grab me. Suddenly his arms froze in midair. His mocking face changed to an expression of horror. Without another word he fled across the quagmire. Never did I find out who he was or what he saw.

One afternoon, to keep from disturbing the family at siesta time, I took my portable typewriter out into the garden to type some choruses for the children's Bible club.

Yvette Pelissier came to see what I was doing. She wanted to try typing and she wanted to learn the choruses. When I explained the purpose of the choruses, she offered to bring many children to the club. Yvette was the junior track champion for all North Africa. Her influence was tremendous among the youth in Megrine. She had no problems fulfilling her promise.

With Yvette's enthusiastic help and the help of our Baptist neighbor and her children, the Bible club prospered. The action choruses made a hit and the novelty of flannelgraph stories held the children spellbound.

After Yvette's first club meeting, we went for a walk. Her daring front was only a cover. Her fingernails, chewed until they had bled, betrayed her insecurity. I attempted to introduce her to God's love through the story of the Good Shepherd and the lost sheep. She listened with unusual interest. Then we returned to Yvette's house where I met her family. Her mother made up in gentleness what she lacked in energy. To be a Jew, she had unusual disinterest in spiritual things. The French father mocked his conversion to Judaism, which he had made simply to win his bride. He confessed to being an atheist. When I asked his permission for his children to attend our Bible club, he said they were free to do as they pleased.

Eventually, the Catholic priest became alarmed. He posted a warning in the Catholic church saying, "There is a young American in Megrine. She has a strange power of persuasion. If you allow her into your home, you will be constrained to believe her false doctrine. Do not accept her visits. Do not allow your children to go to her club."

Suddenly, many homes were closed to me, and many children left the Bible club. Furthermore, the people's suspicions were aroused. They imagined many false stories about me which they circulated among themselves.

One elderly lady refused to shut me out of her house.

She invited me in, saying, "You have never taught false doctrine. You only speak of Jesus. I cannot shut you out of my house."

"Why do you imply you should?" I asked.

She divulged the priest's warning. It surprised me that anyone as insignificant as I could attract the attention of the Catholic church. But I had a nicer surprise. The elderly lady told me a beautiful story.

"I love to hear you talk about Jesus," she said. "Once when I was praying at Jesus' altar in the church, He appeared to me in a vision. He told me my sins were forgiven, and He promised to be with me everywhere I went. He welcomed me always to His altar. Since that day, I feel His presence in my home, in the market, at church, and everywhere. I have never prayed again except at His altar. The people here think I am strange. They do not believe my story."

"I believe your story. I also feel His presence with me always," I said. It was a disconcerting as well as delightful revelation that a Catholic could have experienced Christ in the Catholic church. My prejudiced background had not provided grounds for such a miracle. It was time I re-examined my prejudices.

Yvette was not influenced by the village priest. She accepted Christ and studied the Bible with avidity. Amazingly, her father began to persecute her and even threatened to kill her. His enigmatic behavior contradicted the permission he gave his children to believe as they pleased.

Every time I visited Yvette's home her parents were most hospitable to me. Had Yvette not showed me the marks of the beatings she received, I could not have believed her story. In spite of the daily beatings Yvette received for coming to my house, she came anyway for at least a prayer. Her father's forbidding her did not stop her.

Finally, I decided to confront him about it and went to visit him.

"Hello, Mr. Pelissier," I said. "I especially came to see you today."

"Hello, you are welcome," he replied.

The casual conversation that followed betrayed no change of his attitude. Finally, I said, "Mr. Pelissier, is it true you have forbidden your children to come to my house and you beat them if they do?"

"Yes, I forbid them, and I ask you to drive them away if they go there," he said.

"Mr. Pleissier, I want to apologize if I have hurt you or your family in any way to cause this reaction," I said.

"You haven't done anything. I just don't want them to go, because this religion changes them too much," he replied.

"Did I not frankly tell you that the power of God changes the hearts and lives of the believers," I said.

"Yes, but I didn't believe it. Now please run my children away if they come to your house," he answered.

"Mr. Pelissier, I'm sorry but if your children brave your punishments to come to the Bible club, I shall not drive them away," I affirmed.

Thereupon, Mr. Pelissier rose from his seat, grabbed Yvette by the neck and began to choke her. Not daring to move lest I made matters worse, I expected him to kill her. Yvette's face got red; she could not make a sound. Finally, she fell limp on the floor. Was she dead? I did not know.

Yvette's persecution increased in manner and in intensity until it reached a climax. In February 1954, a Baptist missionary from northwestern Tunisia visited me. She stayed until the last bus returned to Tunis at 8 o'clock in the evening. Returning from escorting her to the bus stop, I met Yvette.

"What are you doing here, Yvette?" I asked.

"My mother warned me to flee from the house. My father has a loaded pistol and he swore he would kill me tonight," she answered.

How I longed to protect this 17-year-old from her brutal father. Still, I knew she needed a much safer refuge than I could ever be. She had to learn to trust God.

"Yvette," I said, "haven't you testified that you are determined to trust God in life or in death? The road ahead demands unshakeable faith to the end. Now you have the opportunity to prove your faith. Your father cannot kill you unless God allows it. If God does allow it, your heavenly Father will receive you."

What a decision! Yvette closed her eyes and clenched her fists. After a brief pause, she relaxed and said, "I'll go home. If I live, I'll live for Christ. If I die, I'll die for Him." We prayed together on the street, then Yvette went home.

In the meantime, Yvette's father had gone out into the streets looking for her. I returned home and told my landlady what was happening. We prayed together for Yvette. At 10 o'clock a knock came at the door. My landlady ran into the kitchen and locked the door. Her children went up under the beds. I longed to flee, too. I stood stiff with fright, but I had to answer the knock. Yvette's father was standing one yard from me with his pistol pointing at my heart.

"Where is Yvette?" he bellowed.

"I do not know. She was on the street at 8 o'clock, and I told her to go home," I answered.

"You have hidden her here. She's a minor, and you have no right to keep her. I'll have you arrested," he shouted.

"Your daughter isn't here. If you are not afraid that the power of God might strike you down if you desecrate my home in any such way, you are free to come in and search," I replied with a great deal more courage than I actually felt.

Turning, he left my door. All the way down the street he shouted curses and threats at me.

Finding Yvette at home, he beat her until she could not stand, stripped her of most of her clothes, and locked her in the kitchen. The following morning he dragged her into his bedroom. With the pistol pointing at her, he said, "Deny this Jesus Christ, or I swear I'll shoot you."

"He is everything to me. I cannot deny him. I wish you knew what a friend He is," she answered.

Turning white with rage, her father tried to pull the trigger, but it was jammed. God did not let him kill her. He chased her from his house at knifepoint. From that day, God gave me the privilege of making a home for Yvette, and He gave us protection from her father.

After Yvette came to live with me, I had to move from the widow's house. Nearby there was a garage that had been divided into two rooms and was offered for rent. That became our home and mission. We lived in the back room and used the front room for worship services.

By that time the Church of God World Missions Department was sending me $50 a month for support. With rent, utilities, groceries and transportation, I had to budget. Occasionally, Yvette and I had to trust God for our next meal.

Once Yvette noticed that we ate our last food for breakfast. It was not time to expect a check from missions. It upset Yvette very much.

"What shall we eat for dinner?" she asked.

"Well, I don't know yet. Why? Are you hungry?" I replied.

"No, but I shall be hungry at noon and we do not have anything to eat," she observed.

"God has plenty of time before dinner to provide us with food," I assured her.

Yvette remained fairly calm until after the postman passed. Occasionally, we would receive a dollar in a letter. When the postman passed and we received no mail at all, Yvette became more agitated.

"There, you see," she said, "no money came in the mail. How do you think God is going to provide for us now?"

"He has unknown resources. He has never failed, and He will not now," I affirmed.

Nervously, Yvette bounced a ball around in tempo with her racing thoughts. The time ticked away.

At 11:30 a truck stopped in front of our door. Maurice, a young Jewish man who occasionally attended our mission, got out. He rushed around to the back of the truck, took out a box, and brought it into the house. He sat it on the table saying, "I'm sorry I have no time to visit with you now. I have to get back to Tunis and close the wholesale grocery by noon. Last night I could not sleep. In a vision, I saw these things which God said I was to put into a box and have them to you before noon today. Goodbye." He was already driving away before we could properly answer him.

A great variety of the finest quality products filled the box. Under the box Maurice had placed 50 francs — equivalent to $15.

While I prepared dinner, I could hear Yvette in the chapel asking God to forgive her for doubting His loving providence.

After some weeks, one morning we were again without food or money. Yvette cautiously concealed her anxiety until after 11:30. Then, she could no longer contain her complaint.

"Doesn't God know we are without food and money?" she exclaimed. "What are we going to eat today?"

"I don't know. He surely will provide if we wait patiently for Him," I said.

"Wait patiently until when?" she answered. "It is almost mealtime already and...Oh, hello, Mr. Boulaire!" she interrupted.

Mr. Boulaire was an elderly French gentleman who re–gularly attended our mission. He asked Yvette to please jump on the bicycle and go to the store for him. His wife wanted something quickly. He was carrying two baskets of produce.

"I just thought you would enjoy some fresh vegetables and fruits from my garden," he said. "I have been work-ing in it all morning and suddenly felt like I should share with you."

Even while I thanked him, I began to wash the vegeta-bles for a tossed salad and fry some of the potatoes and eggplant. After Yvette returned from the store, she knelt in the chapel and repented for her lack of faith. The delicious aroma of fried vegetables drew her to the table. How pre-cious were the Lord's gifts.

Yvette's faith required one last lesson, however, for it to be established. A third time we were without food or money. All morning Yvette could not settle on any activi-ty. She bounced the ball, teased the cat and rode speedily around the quarter on the bicycle Her restlessness betrayed her doubts.

Finally, at 11:55 I said, "I've noticed your neurosity all morning. Do I know what you are thinking?"

"Well, let's just say that you and God will really have to work a miracle if we eat at noon today," she replied.

"God can do it without my help. Let us sit outside and watch from which direction He will supply our need," I challenged.

We walked out the door and saw a lovely Jewish maiden coming towards us with a huge tray on her head.

"Here is some couscous mother sent to you," she called. "We have guests today and I must help serve them so I'll hurry. I hope you enjoy the couscous." She gave us the tray and hurried away.

Couscous is steamed wheatmeal served with stewed meat and vegetables. As the village church clock struck twelve, Yvette and I sat down at the table to eat the delicious, steaming meal.

"Yvette," I teased, "shall we ask God to give us the spoon for eating this lovely food?"

Never again did Yvette doubt God's providence, no matter what the test.

As soon as the check arrived from World Missions, I would plan a budget to stretch it over the month. Twenty-five dollars paid the rent and utilities. Five dollars paid the baker who delivered the bread daily to our door. Ten dollars went for travel, postage and incidentals. Only $10 remained for groceries for the month. With $6 I bought any unperishable staples. Once a week I took a dollar to Tunis to buy vegetables and a little meat. Horsemeat was less expensive than beef or lamb. I could get two extra-thin steaks, one-half kilogram of ground meat and six link sausages for 60 cents. The butcher gave me marrow bones with which I made soup.

Once when I returned from town with the groceries, Yvette called me just as I sat the basket on the table. Our dog, Dicku, was sitting by the table. I warned him not to bother the meat while I was gone. Dicku did not bother anything, but Micki the cat came in. Being less scrupulous than Dicku, Micki stole the link sausages and ran. Hearing the commotion, I got back just in time to see Micki running out the door with Dicku in hot pursuit. Micki carrying the link sausages, Dicku barking and me shouting made an amusing parade that lives on in my memory.

One Saturday in June 1954, Yvette and I were in Tunis. Yvette saw her sports trainer.

"Where have you been, Yvette? You haven't been to the sports club in months. Do you know the races are scheduled for tomorrow? Do come and run. You can beat your own record," he said.

"How can I beat my record. I haven't kept up the training," she retorted.

"But I'm sure that even without training you can do it. You are phenomenal, Yvette. Do please come," he pleaded.

"Maybe I will," she answered. "But I cannot tell you now. I'll just see in the morning."

That night Yvette could not sleep. She finally slipped out of bed about midnight and prayed for several hours. I pretended to sleep to protect her privacy.

The next morning was Pentecost Sunday. I had already made up my mind that if Yvette chose to run in the race on Pentecost Sunday, she would have to wake up early enough without my help. After it was too late for her to take the train, I woke her up for breakfast.

"I've decided to run for the prize of the high calling of God in Christ Jesus. I want to be a champion for Christ like Charles Studd," she said. She had just read Studd's autobiography.

What a sacred service we had that Pentecost Sunday! To make it more special, while we were pronouncing the benediction, a rush of power struck Yvette and spun her around with the speed of a top. She spoke in tongues and could not stop for two hours. Think what she would have missed had she gone to the races.

A few months later a delegation of men from Megrine knocked on my door.

"Good morning, what can I do for you?" I asked.

"We have come to ask some questions. May we come in?" they answered.

"Yes, do come in. I'll try to answer anything you want to ask," I replied.

"We have watched you very closely since you came to Megrine, following you everywhere you went. It is unusual for us to see an unmarried girl living alone. You do not apparently work, yet you have money to live. You can't be rich or you would not live in this garage. We imagined that you were a prostitute or that you were an agent for white slavery, but we have found no evidence to support our suspicions. We despised you, insulted you and slandered you; but you have served us and showed us friendliness. Now, why? Why do you love our people after we have been so inhospitable to you?"

The day before their arrival I had passed the crisis of rejection. God showed me they had not rejected me, but Him. The love in my heart was His love, it was not my own. Without that experience I possibly would not have known how to answer the delegation.

"Oh, is that all you want to know? The answer is simple," I said. "It is God who loves you and your village. My human love would not have endured. His love in me reaches out to bless you and save you to the uttermost."

"We want to bring our families to your prayers," they said. "Do you mind?"

"No, of course, I do not mind. You are welcome every time," I assured them.

The next day 42 people packed into that 9-foot-square room. How they worshipped!

Some time later the villagers crowded into the mission for Sunday worship. With tears streaming down their faces they sang of Calvary. Softly, slowly, they repeated the refrain. When the singing ended and I stood to read the Bible, awesome silence gripped everyone. Suddenly, a burst of power filled the room. I fell to the floor. Visions of glory eclipsed all temporal sights for me. When the power finally left me, I realized that three people were rejoicing in tongues. They had never heard of the baptism in the Holy Spirit and speaking in tongues. One of them was praising in perfect English. Overwhelmed with what God had done, I lifted up my eyes and saw a cloud of exceeding brightness hovering over the room. The Holy Spirit certainly spoke an unmistakable "Amen" to their worship.

In November 1954 Mae Jones arrived in Tunisia. She was more knowledgeable than I about organizing the church work and the outreach program. With our youth participating, we organized visitation programs, youth clubs, and three mission stations. Yvette led the youth services, and Nicolas Buccellato often preached in the mission stations. Mae's influence and practical leadership left their effects when she returned to the United States after nine months.

Life was very difficult for Yvette after her conversion. She braved rejection from her family. Our restricted lifestyle imposed adjustments on her. However, God had a plan for Yvette's happiness. In November 1955 she married a young Christian from our mission.

As I began to teach, I found I had much to learn. The people challenged my doctrine. Jealously, I searched the Scriptures for support of my point of view. When I discovered that the meaning of some scripture verses in English was different from the meaning in the French, Italian or Arabic Bibles, I wrote to my pastor in Anniston, Alabama, disclosing my dilemma.

He replied, "I admit that you possibly cannot support every teaching by the Bible in other languages. You have to encourage the people to accept your teaching out of love for Christ."

Not knowing how to adapt that attitude without adding to the simple Word of God, I decided to concede the point of their challenge. Clearly, I needed to attend more diligently to what the Bible really says. When further challenged by atheistic professors from the University of Paris, Buddhists, occultists and every type of philosopher, I kept an open mind and relied on the Holy Spirit to teach me and to protect me from error. What a security!

After Yvette married and Mae returned to the United States, I depended increasingly on Nicolas' help in the mission. Inevitably, we were attracted to each other. Everything seemed so right for our relationship. He, a staunch believer, was active in the ministry. There were doubts, however. How could I be the kind of missionary I wanted to be and simultaneously be the kind of wife and homemaker I wanted to be? If there were doubts, God and my mission had first claim on my life. The conflict increased in intensity as we shared more and more in the work of the mission.

It was a relief when Mae returned to Tunisia in January 1956. Mae listened to me, advised me tactfully and waited prayerfully.

For eight months Nicolas and I worked with tentative plans to marry. Never finding perfect peace about the plans, I prayed for God to take over and work the whole thing out His way regardless of the cost. Soon after that true relinquishment, Nicolas and I gave up the idea of marriage. He made plans to attend the Bible school in Haiti to prepare for the ministry. It was a painful decision, but I never regretted God's way. In August 1956 Mae returned to the United States, and Nicolas entered the Bible school in Haiti.

The mission work continued to prosper and many people believed on Christ in the following year. The new believers desired to be baptized in water. As a lady minister, I did not have the authority to perform any of the church ordinances. Repeated requests for some male minister to come and baptize the believers brought no results. Finally, I went to Germany to compel someone to come.

My budget trip to Germany consisted of a round trip on the ship from Tunis to Marseille, France, riding on the deck; a round trip on the train from Marseille to Stuttgart, Germany, and 20 marks (German currency) left over. Presumably, the 20 marks were for a hotel room for one night. I planned to go straight to Germany, make my appeal for a minister to come to Tunisia, spend one night, and return straight to Tunisia. It never entered my mind that I could ask our missionaries in Germany to come meet me at the train station. Even less did I expect to be lodged and fed. Although I had extended hospitality to hundreds of acquaintances as well as strangers, I did not presume anyone must do it for me. I was surprised.

After walking from the train station in Winnenden, Germany, to the Church of God, I stood ringing the doorbell. A full day of exposure to the July sun on the ship deck had left my face dreadfully sunburned and a full night of exposure to the damp chilling wind had resulted in a bronchial congestion.

When Bobbie Lauster came to her door, she did not recognize me. I introduced myself, explained my purpose in coming, and requested help in finding a cheap hotel for one night—all in one breath. Bobbie graciously disregarded everything except my introduction. Pulling me into the house, she welcomed me like a long-lost sister.

"A good hot bath will relax you," she said. "Then, you need a hot meal. We have just eaten, but there is plenty of warm food left. You can eat all you want. After that you will enjoy lounging in a lawn chair under our cherry trees in the backyard. The cherries are perfect for eating at this time of year and the trees are loaded. You will have a room here to stay as long as you desire, and we'll have plenty of time to discuss what you came for after you have rested."

Such unexpected graciousness overwhelmed me. Well experienced in handling adversity with composure, I lost all composure when treated kindly. How grateful I was when she left me alone. Was she really too busy to stay with me? Was she simply wise enough to discern that I would be embarrassed to reveal my total lack of composure?

After showing me my room and the kitchen, she led me to the bathroom where Gisela, a lovely German girl, was already preparing a steaming bath. Then, I was left alone.

Safely shut into the bathroom I released my tears. All the five years of suffering and loneliness, combined with the wearisome trip I had just made, dissolved in tears and washed me internally while the hot bath relaxed my aching muscles. The prolonged bath provided time for the traces of my uncontrollable weeping to disappear.

Venturing out of the bathroom, I found the table set for one in the kitchen. Delicious southern style food was steaming on the stove. "We have already eaten," Bobbie had said. "There is plenty of food; eat all you want." For five years I had eaten native foods, all cooked in olive oil and hot with pepper. My palate relished the southern-style vegetables and cornbread. Freely, hungrily, I consumed the delectable food. The bread, olives and cheese that I had brought from Tunisia to economize the expense of restaurants were forgotten. Bobbie certainly had mastered culinary art.

After washing my dishes, I timidly sneaked out to the backyard, still fearing a new emotional outburst. A lounge chair with pillows and a blanket had been prepared for me. Books, magazines, and a huge bowl of cherries were on a table nearby. No one disturbed my rest in that splendid pastoral setting. The pure air and calm landscape healed and strengthened me. My mind and body could scarcely absorb such luxury.

Bobbie called the American servicemen's wives. They bought me some warm clothes and paid my expenses to a conference in Karlsruhe, conducted by Evangelist Tommy Hicks. I accepted an invitation to share my testimony at a German convention, where I appealed for someone to come to Tunisia. As a result of the appeal, two ministers agreed to come to Tunisia to conduct a revival and to baptize the believers. As a bonus, Elfrieda Wagner, Gisela's sister, dedicated her life to God for missions. To run my cup over, I received an airline ticket back to Tunisia and over 1,000 marks to help with the expenses of the coming revival.

In mid-August, Lambert DeLong and Lamar McDaniel arrived in Tunisia. They preached nightly with me interpreting. They baptized all the believers and organized the church. This energetic young church was destined to scatter seeds of faith in places far removed from Megrine.

Chapter 10

TRANSITIONS

*M*y last years in Tunisia were characterized by constant change. Everyone was affected by the political upheavals and the changes.

The Church of God World Missions Board had been observing my activities for several years. Since they partially supported me, they proposed to appoint me as a missionary.

My first reaction to the proposition was negative. I loved my church and was loyal to it, but I could not understand any advantage in changing my status. God had provided all my needs for guidance and support.

Then God rebuked me. "Do not despise the instrument I choose to use. This is the way I've planned for you. For your own protection, walk in it," He counseled.

"I trust you, God," I prayed. "I do not want to get out of your plan, for then I would be on my own. I am not wise enough to walk alone. Protect me from presumption and from arrogance. I'll submit to the Missions Board in your name. Please, God, give me the assurance that you will always direct their decisions where they pertain to me." With that guidance and confidence, I received missionary status on April 20, 1956.

Being a missionary under appointment by the Church of God provided me protection from arrogance and doctrinal error. I valued that protection, as I valued the basic nurturing I received from the Church of God through my formative years. God's ways are perfect; in them is security.

When Nicolas went to Haiti, his mother and sister were left with no means of support. I invited them to come live with me. Rosy, Nicolas' sister, found employment in a cookie factory nearby. Mamina took over all the housekeeping. She spoiled Rosy and me in every way. The 18 months with them were the happiest of my life.

Relieved of all domestic responsibilities and finding increasing assistance from the youth in the mission, I developed the mission program. During the day I did my correspondence and bookkeeping. At night I found relaxation visiting the members. I laughed much in those days. The wholesome, simple pleasures balanced the sober responsibilities in a manner that was never recaptured after Mamina and Rosy left me and moved to Italy.

During this time *The Greatest Thing in the World*, by Henry Drummond, crashed into my life. All my past spiritual experience had prepared me for the revolutionary challenge of this book. Finding it the logical sequel to my deliverance from legalism, I accepted its message into the vacuum that was in my heart. Thoroughly I devoured the teaching, memorizing it, and apprehending it in my daily experience. All my relationships and my teachings revealed its influence.

This period saw spiritual growth in our mission. A new

assembly that we opened in Tunis developed keen spiritual awareness. We enjoyed unprecedented freedom to witness. When I left Tunisia in March 1958 for my first furlough, a healthy group of local Christians assumed responsibility for the continuation of the services.

It was a delight to be home after six years in North Africa. Everything at home seemed so different at first. Nothing was as I had left it. Finally, I realized the major changes were within me, not in the home situation.

Those changes affected my meeting with the World Missions Board. The dignity and wisdom of the board members commanded my utmost respect and reverence. Nevertheless, I was not intimidated as in my first meeting with them seven years previously. Freely, I gave a report of the mission activities in Tunisia and answered the board's numerous questions. Just before I was dismissed, the chairman asked me, "What would be your reaction, Sister Gaines, if the board did not agree to send you back to Tunisia?"

I am sure the question was valid and without malice. My reply was honest and sincere. I answered, "Gentlemen, we are living in an age when everyone is conscious of his rights in the home, in the government and in the religious community. I relinquished all my rights for one God-given right. That is to preach the gospel on the foreign field. I'm not the least afraid that right will be taken away."

"Does that mean you will defy the Missions Board?" I was asked.

Remembering that I had trusted God to direct every decision of the World Missions Board where it pertained to me, I confidently answered, "I really do not know why you ask me this. I can only reply that my trust in God is such that I do not expect such an eventuality."

Whatever deliberation followed, I was permitted to

return to Tunisia with full missionary status, for which I was humbly grateful. Upon my return to Tunisia, I found the mission flourishing in spite of a great threat rising on the horizon.

Tunisia's struggle for independence, which first erupted the day I booked passage to North Africa in 1952, steadily intensified. Guerilla attacks daily ravaged Tunis. I narrowly escaped explosions on several occasions. Stores were gutted. Even the American Cultural Center and the American Consulate were attacked. Finally, the climax came. France relinquished its hold on Tunisia.

In 1956 Tunisia celebrated its independence. Tunisian nationals rejoiced exuberantly, whereas anyone claiming French or Italian citizenship suddenly was considered an alien. It would take some time for the new regime to sti– pulate their rights and limitations.

The French employed in government positions were the first to suffer the transition. Tunisian nationals succeeded to their positions, resulting in the expulsion of these displaced persons to France. Gradually, this trend spread to everyone except industrialists or small business owners. Laws whereby Tunisian nationals held controlling interest in all business and industry were proposed. The resulting dissatisfaction and readjustments proved more than many industrialists chose to endure. Consequently, there followed a tremendous exodus of Europeans from Tunisia.

Our church families were also affected. Steadily our members transferred to Europe. From 1957 to 1961 our church was composed of a constantly changing stream of newcomers.

Even after gaining independence, Tunisia struggled with France, who refused to relinquish her naval base in Ferryville. More guerilla attacks were initiated against the French. Border clashes with Algeria increased tensions.

The climax came when France airlifted foreign legion paratroopers and staged a devastating attack on Tunisian resistants in Ferryville and Bizerte. The brutal attack was out of proportion to the revolt of the sparsely armed and totally untrained masses of Tunisians. The alarming casualty toll ignited the nationals' demand for vengeance. No foreigner in Tunisia felt secure. Only the French agreement to relinquish its naval base in Ferryville cooled the boiling Tunisian blood.

During this time several missionaries were expelled from the country on 48 hours notice. Among them were my friends from northwestern Tunisia. As tension increased, the solidarity of the fundamental missionaries strengthened.

Unrelenting stress aggravated the amoebic dysentery that I had barely kept under control for five years. The disease prostrated me and threatened my life. I plainly had reached a crossroads. Weighing all these circumstances, the Church of God World Missions Board decided that I should transfer to France.

Ten of the best years of my life had been spent in Tunisia. I loved Tunisia from the first day until the end. My senses thrilled to its folklore. When I boarded the ship for my final departure, the police officer said, "You seem to be leaving permanently. Why? You know we are not expelling you. You are one of us." No, they did not expel me, and I was the doyenne of American missionaries in Tunisia at the time of my departure. I felt the oneness with the Tunisian people. It was a difficult parting for me. Without understanding, I nevertheless accepted the will of God and moved to Europe.

Europe delights every romanticist or historian. Every European country provides a wealth of sources for historical research and cultural enlightenment. Inevitably, I loved my new home, but not without reservations.

Historical research and cultural enlightenment were secondary to my missionary calling. Europeans could better accomplish anything I could do in Europe. Realizing I was superfluous, I purposed only to re-establish contact with friends who had transferred from Tunisia. Introducing them to new church homes in their vicinity became my objective. Because the people were scattered all over France, Italy and Switzerland, it took much traveling to achieve my aim. Consequently, most of my sojourn in Europe was spent on the highways.

My residence was established in Troyes. Mrs. Henriette Guerland, a member of our church, lived alone in a five-room apartment. She had been divinely healed of a serious heart disease and was emerging from a paralyzing depression. She was thrilled to rent me a room. Together we redecorated her apartment. In our mutual need, a deeply affectionate mother-daughter relationship evolved. Unto her death in 1976 that relationship held strong.

My physical condition worsened steadily. Also, having contacted everyone I could find from Tunisia, I had no further worthwhile employment that I was able to perform. When I could ignore the impasse no longer, I purposed to pray through about it. "Praying through," in Pentecostal jargon, implied prevailing in prayer until a clear solution to a problem had been revealed.

Walter and Bobbie Lauster had been transferred from Winnenden to oversee the Church of God in the Saarland and France. They left me in charge of their home and the secretarial responsibilities of the area while they were on furlough in the United States. In their living room I knelt alone to pray about my future.

"God," I prayed, "I'm ready to live or I'm ready to die. I'm not prepared to abide in this state of living death. Heal me of this amoebic dysentery or kill me." Never before had I been so desperately definite.

God had the answer ready, but my own emotions created so much static I had to pray through them before I could hear. Eventually, the Holy Spirit prayed through me in tongues. My spirit relaxed. My striving ceased. The Holy Spirit prophesied: "You shall live and not die. You shall still serve me in a distant land. This shall be your sign: you will receive two letters. They will be written on the same day on separate sides of the world. You will receive them on the same day. They will reveal my plan for you."

Three days later two letters arrived. One was from the World Missions Board. The second was from Jerusalem. I opened the letter from Jerusalem first, as I had never before received a letter from the Holy Land. and it intrigued me.

George Kuttab, Church of God overseer in Jordan, expressed his pleasure that I should soon be joining the staff in Jerusalem. My assistance in the Christian day school on the Mount of Olives was greatly anticipated.

Our Executive Missions Secretary wrote that the World Missions Board had decided that my experience with Arabs in Tunisia and my knowledge of the Arabic language would prove beneficial to the missionary endeavors in Jordan. Would I accept to be transferred to Jerusalem?

Only after I read the second letter did I realize that they had been written from separate sides of the world, dated the same day, and although they were delayed more than two weeks, they both reached me on the same day. The Spirit of God witnessed with my spirit that these were the letters of which I had been informed. I accepted their message as God's plan for my life, and I agreed to the transfer.

The plans for my future both excited me and calmed me, but my physical condition remained unchanged. During the following weeks I cooked for the Pioneers for Christ, a witnessing group from the United States, but I could eat only unseasoned boiled rice, plain yogurt, grilled lean meat and apple juice. This diet, which I had scrupulously maintained for more than two years, had not healed me. Nevertheless, if I deviated from it in the least, an attack of dysentery would reduce my body weight by 30 pounds in three days. That condition changed instantly.

In the German camp meeting in July 1963, God miraculously healed me. While praying, I sensed God speaking to my inner being saying that I was healed and I could safely eat anything. That same evening I went home and ate a bacon and tomato sandwich and slept soundly the whole night with no ill effects. My strength steadily increased from that moment.

In the fall of 1963 I returned to the United States for a brief furlough before making final plans to move to Jordan. It was a special furlough. I saw my sister Ruth for the first time in 22 years. For the first time in 17 years, I saw Florence. It was my last visit with my father and my last Christmas to be with my family. Friends that I made on this trip while on deputation in the Northwest and Western Canada would prove to be faithful supporters who would correspond with me for many years. The short furlough produced precious memories. I welcomed the return to my mission, nevertheless. In February I returned to France to prepare for my move to Jordan.

Characteristically oblivious to the problems, I planned to drive my Simca 1000 to Jordan. Consequently, I needed transit visas for Yugoslavia, Greece, Turkey, Syria and Lebanon before departure. Switzerland and Italy required no transit visas for American citizens. Also, in order to transfer my furniture to Jordan, a temporary residence visa was required. Obtaining these visas would take a week in Paris.

The first week of March 1964 was prematurely warm in Troyes. I did not foresee a hasty return of winter weather, so I drove to Paris with light woolen clothing. Although it took all day Monday to drive to Paris and get settled in an inexpensive hotel, I had obtained all the visas by Thursday except for the one for Syria. The Syrian Consulate required an affidavit proving my religious status before issuing a visa. When I returned to the Syrian Consulate with the required document, the office was closed. In unbelief I stood staring at the locked door. Would I really have to stay over the weekend in Paris for this one visa? The weather had turned freezing cold, and snow had begun to fall. What if winter storms blocked me here indefinitely? All for one visa!

"Can I help you?" pleasantly spoke a stranger.

"No, I guess you can't since this office is closed until Monday and I want a visa," I answered.

"Do come in. I do not promise I'll help you, but I can try. The lady who issues visas has the necessary stamps locked in her desk and she keeps the keys. She is off today but I'll search the entire office for stamps. If I find them, I'll issue your visa. It would be unfortunate for you to be delayed in Paris three days extra only for a visa," he replied.

I could not believe what I heard. Why should this man exert himself for a stranger? I followed him inside. He conscripted every employee in the consulate to search for stamps. With patience and time the stamps were found and my visa was issued. Everyone wished me a safe journey and begged me to deliver their fond greetings to their beloved homeland. For my part, I will always cherish my happy, first impression of Syria and Syrians because of that unselfish employee at the consulate.

On rainy March 10, 1964, I drove out of Troyes for the last time—destination Jerusalem. My first stop was Basel, Switzerland. The overseer of the Church of God in Europe and the Middle East, Vessie Hargrave, lived there. He advised me to take more money with me, as I only had a meager $110. My stubborn independence constrained me to refuse a loan from him. I did promise to call him for assistance in case of an emergency, which promise I did not keep.

From Basel I went to Lausanne to see Yvette and tell her goodbye. Yvette and her family had been in Lausanne, Switzerland, since they left Tunisia.

Swinging back to southern France, I bade farewell to many acquaintances, most of whom had been in Tunisia previously. Finally, I crossed northern Italy. Entering Yugoslavia at Trieste, I drove through Yugoslavia to Greece. In Greece I contacted many lovely Christians. From Thessalonica to Athens, the Greeks showed me warm hospitality, forming cherished memories.

Car trouble devoured part of my money. By the time I returned to Thessalonica from Athens, I knew I would never have enough money to reach Jerusalem. Pride kept me from calling Brother Hargrave. Independence hindered my requesting any assistance from Greek friends. Finally, I went to the American Consulate to cash a personal check. The staff declined to do so, saying that it was not their policy. An American, who was living and working in Thessalonica, offered on his own to stand security for my check if I wanted to cash it at the American Express. I had done as much many times for others, but I was amazed that this stranger would do it for me. Until today I appreciate that man.

My marvelous experiences on my trip from Paris through many countries until I reached Jerusalem is a beautiful story in its own right. Everywhere I met the kindest, most helpful people. My confidence in humanity was greatly enhanced.

Early in my trip I learned not to reveal my final destination because it caused too much time-consuming controversy. It was unbelievable to most people in 1964 that I was driving alone from Paris to Jerusalem. Those who actually believed me declared that I must be mentally imbalanced to undertake such a trip. I really was not crazy or courageous, only ignorant. It would take courage for me to make the trip again under the same circumstances.

In the afternoon of April 2, 1964, I arrived in Jerusalem. From many years of Bible study, I knew the Mount of Olives was on the east of the city. With no problem I drove straight to the church.

The Rev. and Mrs. George Kuttab were in Bethlehem for midweek services. Their children were at home alone. I explained to the children who I was, and I promised to contact their parents in the evening. Then, I went to reserve a room in a simple hotel. The long, incredible trip had thoroughly exhausted me. I definitely needed a good night's rest in a private room before I began adjustments to my new land.

Fortunately for me, I could never guess the trauma of discovering the Holy Land.

Chapter 11

Slow It Down, Margaret

Past experiences had prepared me for Jordan. I did not know how to appropriate these experiences, but God knew. He selected episodes from my past and pointed out their relevance to immediate situations. Patiently, He reshaped me to my new land.

How absurd to have expected my experience with Tunisian Arabs to equip me for establishing wholesome relationships with the Jordanians and Palestinians! Their social and philosophical differences mocked my alleged competence. Likewise, my inadequate knowledge of Tunisian Arabic handicapped me more than it helped me. Desperately trying to shut Tunisian grammar and usage out of my mind, I applied myself aggressively to classical Arabic. It would take nine years of dogged study before I would achieve fluency.

My personal immaturities invariably posed more obstacles for me than the language and people did. Consciously, I entered Jordan as a teacher. Not surprisingly, I remained there as a student.

Even after 12 years on the mission field, I was still too impulsive. I had to learn to accept God's timing. A fierce perfectionist, it was imperative that I develop appreciation for the imperfect. Still too talkative, I had to "study to be quiet." My exaggerated need to right wrongs had to be exposed for what it was—playing God. That constituted a formidable syllabus. Life's vicissitudes would be the teacher.

Immediately after my arrival in Jerusalem, I was challenged with a problem. The Jordanian customs asked $1,000 in cash for duties for my car. Incredible! The car only cost $1,100 new. Where was I to get the cash? What could I do without a car? Besides, I would receive very little cash if I sold it. What were the possibilities of trading it in on a new car? Everything I tried to do failed, but the problem could not be ignored.

My mind and body could not function properly to cope with the challenge. The long, tiresome trip from France, during which I slept little and ate only what I could prepare quickly on a tiny alcohol lamp, had totally exhausted me. I instinctively rebelled against everything. I aggravated the situation by forcing myself to reject my rebellion in an effort not to make an intolerable first impression on my colleagues.

Just before the deadline for my decision concerning the car, Kash Amburgy's tour group came to Jerusalem. The spiritual encouragement and the refreshing fellowship I received from these lovely Christians steadied me to face the perplexities ahead. Mary Lou Amburgy accepted my burden with me during that encounter, and she has faithfully carried it with me until now.

After I decided to trade the Simca 1000 for a new car, an evangelist came and begged me to sell him the Simca. For two hours I tried to explain to him that I did not want to sell him the car, I had already decided to trade it. He got several ministers to plead with me to sell it to him for the sake of the gospel at a lower price than I had been offered. Despairing of prevailing against the ministers and, against my better judgment, I finally accepted. The evangelist gave me a check that was not negotiable, and it was a month before he came to pay me for the car. When he did, he gave me less than I had asked because of repairs he had to make on the car. Brother Kuttab could see his point of view better than mine. I felt betrayed, confused and lonely. What an interesting initiation to the Holy Land.

My second challenge came from a clash between Eastern and Western cultures. Wives and all women of an Arab household obey the men explicitly. They would not think of doing anything or going anywhere without permission. It took me several weeks really to understand that I would be expected to obey the men and submit to them like the Arab women. When I finally recognized the obvious, I reacted.

According to his own customs, Brother Kuttab legitimately expressed anger when I went to the post office without asking his permission. I told him his customs and traditions would not be binding on me. I was not a member of his household and neither the church nor the government required that type of subjugation. It would take months before I could define the boundaries of my freedoms and limitations. In the process I made blunders and created resentments that left ugly scars. Worst of all, in the face of the Arab self-control, I always felt like someone was hassling me in a market place. Even when I got a bargain, I suspected that by some unknown principle I had been taken in.

The Middle Eastern code of ethics contrasted to the ethics I had learned. The modesty of dress, morality and hospitality surpassed anything I had ever experienced. I admired the high standards and adopted them as my own. Thousands of times through the years I have praised God for the privilege of living in the protective company of the Arabs, because of these principles. I am deeply indebted to them, but the surprising concepts of honesty in word and deed and what actually constitutes a lie, theft, or a deception still startle me. I am amazed at how a person can presume upon another's resources and time to the point of slave driving, so it seems, without the slightest consciousness that such behavior imposes upon the rights of others or even inconveniences them. Does a Westerner ever really adjust to the Eastern mind, or do they simply resign with varying degrees of resentment?

Coping with the concept of community property is probably the most difficult challenge of all. What is meant by community property deserves more explanation. It is not public property such as roads, schools, post offices and security buildings. If I have a refrigerator, everyone who does not have one has the right to use mine. If I have a car, everyone who does not have one expects to ride in mine whenever it goes. If I have a television, everyone who does not have one has the right to watch mine as long as they choose. Private property belongs to anyone who thinks he needs it. In modern Israel this concept seems to be absurd and exaggerated; however, in the small villages where I have lived, it is a custom practiced to this day. Westerners nearly lose their minds before they learn to cope with such a concept. I was not an exception.

The beauty of these Eastern ideas and practices is that they provide the ideal exercises for training the impulsive to be deliberate, for teaching the talkative the futility of discussion and for proving to the perfectionist that there is rest in relinquishing to imperfection. They also teach that it is sheer suicide to play God.

It is unthinkable that I should find the Eastern culture so exasperating without a realization that my Western culture has a similar effect on the Eastern people. The major difference was that they tolerated me with a great deal of grace, so much so, in fact, that I was slow to realize when I really plagued their spirits. My perfectionist, God-playing roles probably came nearer to driving them to distraction than anything else. It was in the day school that it showed up first.

Inefficiently organized, under staffed, and poorly housed, the school could scarcely be successful at its best. With frustrated, unwilling teachers who emptied their frustrations out on the children daily by unmerciful beatings, it was doomed to be worse than a failure. Too-talkative-impulsive-critical perfectionist that I was, I attacked the school with no restraint except a weak effort to practice the love that *The Greatest Thing in the World* had imposed on me. What a confusing concoction of human reaction I must have projected. The patient, tolerant, self-control that the Arabs portrayed in return belied the resentment and even rebellion I stirred up.

By midsummer I had achieved some bewildering goals. The school was closed—the only positive result of my reactions—and the people turned me off. Some of them slyly referred to me in their sermons by telling stories of how "a queen who is allowed to rule for one day will destroy a kingdom." Obviously, Brother Kuttab and his family had all the sympathy of the Arab world. I had the confrontation with my own failures and the subsequent rejection, without even having the wisdom and the discernment to understand why. Had they been any people other than Arab, I could never have hoped to redeem myself. However, magnanimity of spirit is another of the Arabs' valuable graces.

All of the summer of 1964 I was graciously received and generously served, but also rejected. When I finally realized this fact, I learned to be quieter and to pray secretly.

Challenged by the nature of the adjustments I was required to make, I completely lost my equilibrium. When I resorted to secret prayer, I found that I was too distracted to pray. Initially, I disciplined my body and my mind to observe an act of reverent presence before the throne of grace even if I could not pray. I practiced this discipline two hours a day for three weeks before God succeeded in breaking through my self-made obstacles and poured out on me the real grace of prayer. After I could finally pray, I continued three months in secret prayer before God created the circumstances that would draw Mrs. Kuttab into prayer with me. Some weeks later Brother Kuttab also joined us.

By that time God had succeeded in harnessing my impetuous spirit enough for me to benefit from a textbook: *My Utmost For His Highest*, by Oswald Chambers. The positive challenge which dominates each lesson of this devotional book suited my disposition. Its clear language taught me how to identify my spiritual needs. My spiriual muscles contracted in response. A unique learning experience began then that I still have not exhausted.

Barbara Jensen gave me the book. Her friendship was a rare gift from God.

In January 1965 Barbara, a Lutheran charismatic, visited the Holy Land with her girlfriend. Having encountered some unusual and unpleasant experiences with some missionaries they had met, they mutually agreed to evade all missionaries for the remainder of their trip. Nevertheless, God brought us together. Barbara stayed with me a month. She returned on two other occasions for prolonged work holidays in the Holy Land. The last time, she and her husband worked with me six profitable weeks before they returned to their business in Minneapolis, Minnesota. Their tremendous capacity to love and to serve with utmost humility demonstrated the gospel. The villagers will never forget them.

During Barbara's first trip to the Holy Land, Brother and Sister Kuttab finally began to unite with me in prayer for enlightenment and revival. God responded by giving us startling self-knowledge. Divine light revealed the revival-hindering faults which belonged to each of us. Each one was challenged to bring self to the Cross. The anointing rested upon our work in the measure that we honestly did this. Our relationship was healed and God gave revival. Out of the revival came dedicated young men and women whom we grouped for special training.

Dr. Robert O'Bannon, Church of God overseer of the Middle East, organized the Middle East Theological Institute. The name sounded presumptuous at the time. From today's vantage point, the name seems to have been too modest. The students studied theology, which justified the name, but the practical working out of faith and discipline in daily experience constituted even greater training.

The students enrolled in the institution with the erroneous idea that physical labor is inappropriate for scholars. After their initial astonishment at seeing Dr. O'Bannon as willing to work as he was to teach, the young men joyfully followed his example. Together, they dug a cistern. The young ladies worked with me—washing, shopping, cooking and cleaning. Gradually, the students warmed to the schedule of worship, study, work and recreation. What a happy family we were!

The second term of the Middle East Theological Institute continued its tradition. Dr. O'Bannon planned the schedule and the curriculum. He provided for the teachers and then left for the United States to attend the General Assembly. The supervision of the school was left to me.

I had been living in Amman, Jordan, for seven months. When I returned to Jerusalem to supervise the new term of school, there was an error in my address. The secretaries in the World Missions Department confused my post office box number in Amman with the city of Jerusalem. Consequently, for the entire summer I received no support for the school and no salary. When our support failed to arrive, I sensed that God had added to our curriculum His own course in faith. I thrilled at the prospect, but I concealed our plight from the students and the faculty.

One Friday when I had only 50 cents left, I secretly wondered how God was going to provide. The Rev. Kemp, a professor from Jordan, had completed teaching a course and was about to return home. "Sister Margaret," he said, "if you are short on finances, I can let you borrow a little money. I've saved up some for a vacation my wife and I hope to make later this summer. You could use it."

I was surprised at his proposition, since no one knew our need. Nevertheless, I felt like it would be a breach of faith for me to borrow money. I believed that God had a plan to provide without my having to make a debt and that He would increase the faith of the students. So letting that wonderful opportunity for help escape, I said, "Thank you so much for your offer, Reverend Kemp. I shall certainly remember that, and should I really get into an impasse, I'll call on you." Brother Kemp returned to Amman and would not be back for two weeks.

As I was walking out the door to take our students to Bethlehem for some inservice training, the telephone rang.

"Hello, I am Margaret Gaines," I answered.

"Hello, Margaret. I am Olyda Overgaard, conductor of the Eye-O-Graphic tour to the Holy Land," she said. "Our friend Barbara Jensen told us about you and said we simply have to meet you. When can we see you?"

"I am leaving just now for Bethlehem. Our students will have their evening meal followed by evening devotions and sharing. I do not rush the students in devotions and sharing. They could be finished by 8 o'clock or they may not finish until 10 o'clock. If you do not mind my coming to your hotel as late as that, I should be delighted," I replied.

That evening at 9 o'clock I met Olyda Overgaard for

the first time. Since then, she and many of the pilgrims she has brought on tour have been our prayer partners.

The first meeting was unique. "I really did not intend to contact you so soon," she said. "Our group will return to the United States next week. Christine, my assistant, and I shall stay on for a few days. We planned to see you then, but this morning I felt such an urgency to contact you that I could not wait."

She handed me a gift from Barbara. Glancing inside the imitation leather Bible case I saw 15 dinars—the equivalent of $40. It was not even a check, but cash which could be used immediately. I wanted to shout for joy because of God's marvelous provision, and I did cry, but I controlled my exuberance. To divulge the importance of the gift before the tour group would smack of a subtle solicitation for more help.

"When your tour group leaves, come over and visit us," I invited. "You can see our church from here. Maybe by that time you will want to wash some clothes, or you will be ready for some American-style food. Plan to come over. Then, I shall explain why you felt so much urgency to contact me today."

The following week when Miss Overgaard and Christine spent the day with us, I shared with them and with the students how God had chosen to use these lovely Episcopalian and Lutheran charismatics to provide for our need. Our students had never experienced living by faith. I promised to keep them informed of our financial state, thereafter, so they could enjoy watching and praying with me for God's provision. For the remainder of the term, dramatic providential supply inspired our students to trust God fully. The unique discipline experienced in the two summer terms of Bible school produced several ministers. Those extraordinary young men went on to receive their degrees in other colleges, and they are in the ministry today. How could we have known then the magnificent results of such small beginnings?

In November 1966 the ever-intensifying squabbles between the Arabs and the Israelis resulted in Israel's attack on Sammu village near Hebron. In retaliation the Moslem leaders called for a Jihad or Holy War. Civil defense training began immediately. We painted our car lights blue and taped our windows. Fear mixed with frenzied nationalism dominated our emotions. Everyone knew what was inevitable. No one knew when or how it would erupt.

When King Hussein went to Egypt and consolidated his loyalty to Egypt and the Arab nations in event of an attack from Israel, everyone relaxed. "Now there will be no war," they exclaimed. "Israel would never attack the united Arab front. If she doesn't attack, neither shall the Arabs. So war now is unlikely."

Rejoicing in their false expectations, the Jordanians relaxed their seven-month alert. I did not share their enthusiasm. For a whole week I felt impressed with the following song:

Be Still My Soul

Be still, my soul! the Lord is on thy side;

Bear patiently the cross of grief or pain;

Leave to thy God to order and provide;

In every change He faithful will remain.

Be still, my soul! thy best, thy heavenly Friend

Thro' thorny ways leads to a joyful end.

Be still, my soul! thy God doth undertake

To guide the future as He has the past.

Thy hope, thy confidence let nothing shake;

All now mysterious shall be bright at last.

Be still, my soul! the waves and winds still know

His voice who ruled them while He dwelt below.

Be still, my soul! the hour is hastening on

When we shall be forever with the Lord,

When disappointment, grief, and fear are gone,

Sorrow forgot, love's purest joys restored.

Be still, my soul! when change and tears are past,

All safe and blessed we shall meet at last.

— Katharina von Schlegel

With this lovely hymn came the certainty that war was imminent. On Sunday, June 5, 1967, I shattered the congregation's expectations for peace.

"Do not expect peace," I warned. "This is the last time we shall worship in this sanctuary before it is hit by bombs. Before next Sunday war will break out and disperse us. Some of you will not survive. Prepare to face the issue."

The prophecy seemed insane, but the people believed it. In our congregation there was a judge's wife. She went home and told her husband. He, in turn, shared the prophecy with another judge who was his colleague. The second judge exclaimed, "I fully believe the prophecy. I shall take my family immediately and flee to Amman." The first judge followed him early the next morning.

Elizabeth Van Heamstra and her assistant, Margaret, attended our church. They rented a part of the home of the

Rev. Mattar, custodian of the Garden Tomb. When they informed him of their plans to leave for Holland for the duration of the impending war, he curtly ridiculed them for believing there would be a war. Turning to me he said, "You are not planning to leave, are you, Miss Gaines? What do you think about this nonsense?"

"No, I do not plan to leave," I assured him. "Whether or not Elizabeth's and Margaret's leaving is nonsense is between them and God. As for the war, it shall surely come this very week," I added.

Elizabeth and Margaret left at 6 o'clock on Monday evening. Elizabeth departed on such short notice that she did not have time to plan for taking her dog with her. She left Kevin, a Berner Senna, in my care until she returned. Elizabeth and Margaret were already too late to catch their scheduled flight. They eventually flew out of the Tel Aviv airport in Israel.

By 10 o'clock Monday morning the thunderous explosion of bombs and artillery, followed by smoke and fire, left no doubt that the city of peace was again the scene of a bitter war.

Chapter 12

WONDERFULLY KEPT

Selective forgiveness is an amazing gift. Recalling joy intensifies the very sensations of the joyful experience. Happy moments can be preserved forever in our memory, but pain and distress fade from memory. Overwhelmingly distressful experiences can be recalled, but the sensations of the experience, dying their natural death, refuse to be resurrected.

Numerous and varied were the distresses of 1967. God allowed me to be pushed to the limit of my physical and emotional endurance. He held me there at breaking-point until just before I shattered; then, He released me. How can I remember the pain adequately to express it if, indeed, such intensity of suffering can be verbalized?

From the beginning of the year, the threat of war and intense preparation for it sat us on a political powder-keg. High emotional tensions influenced conversation, work and even the music on the radio. In these situations

Christian missionaries are almost always suspected of being collaborators with the enemy. In my situation as a Christian missionary and a foreigner living alone on the Mount of Olives, I often overheard the antagonistic remarks and threats from my neighbors who passed my window unaware that I was inside. The fact that my relationship with Brother Kuttab was strained by misunderstandings arising from his personal problem with the church supported the suspicion of my Arab friends and resulted in my increased isolation.

In May a letter from home informed me that my father had not recovered from influenza suffered in March. He was in the hospital undergoing examinations to establish a diagnosis. A fearful premonition that my father had a fatal disease hovered over me night and day.

The warning letters from the American Counsul advising all unessential Americans to evacuate the area began to arrive. Not knowing whether or not I would be allowed to stay in Jerusalem during the war, I moved all my furniture to Bethlehem for storage. Our plan was to stay together in Bethlehem in case of war and open a first aid center in the Church of God there. Our building was big enough, and Mrs. Kuttab and Mrs. Amad, Brother Kuttab's sister, were registered nurses.

The outbreak of hostilities caught Mrs. Kuttab with me in the church on the Mount of Olives. Brother Kuttab was on a trip to Germany. The Kuttab children were alone in Bethlehem. The location of the church on the western flank of the Mount of Olives provided a ringside seat for observing the progress of the conflict in Jerusalem. With the welfare of the children tormenting our thoughts, we waited until two in the afternoon. Finally, I got a telephone message through to the American Consul.

"This is Margaret Gaines calling from the Church of God on the Mount of Olives. Our pastor's wife is blocked here, and her five children, including a nursing baby, are alone in Bethlehem. We are going to try to get to Bethlehem," I informed him.

"The major battle is on the Bethlehem road. I advise you to stay where you are," he said.

"Would I be permitted to go at my own risk?" I inquired.

"Yes, if no one stops you. But I hope you fully understand the risks," came the answer.

"I intend to risk it, so for your record in case someone is looking for me, I shall be in Bethlehem," I replied.

After praying for special protection, Mrs. Kuttab, Kevin the dog, and I got into my Volkswagen and set out on our adventurous trip. Knowing the back roads well, I skirted the shortest Bethlehem road, taking the route through Abu Dis, through the Judean desert and into Bethlehem by Shepherds Field.

In Abu Dis two men waved us to a stop. They were fathers frantically trying to get back to their families in Bethlehem. We understood their emotion. Thinking it was just as well for us to have some men along, I agreed to take them. They stared cautiously at Kevin. The Berner Senna breed of dog is related to the Saint Bernard and it is just as big. The two men had to find a way to share the back seat of a Volkswagen with Kevin. It was obvious they hoped Kevin would not object. I assured them that Kevin was extremely gentle and they need not fear. Barely outside the range of the artillery in the desert, we could clearly see the fierce fighting at Government House, headquarters of the United Nations. Several times that day Government House was conquered and reconquered by the Israeli and Jordanian armies locked in a fierce contest for the area.

All along the way the roads were full of refugees fleeing from the immediate battle zone to Jericho or even to the east bank of Jordan. Forced to share war's destructive situation, lifelong enemies laid aside their grievances and devoted themselves to their mutual survival. Any sensitive, caring human being could not witness such a display of human suffering and remain unshaken. Arriving gratefully in Bethlehem and finding the children safe, we nevertheless suffered the agonies of the fleeing refugees and wondered if they had found some refuge and if they would ever return to their land.

Church members living in Jehoshephat Valley facing our church in Jerusalem had watched as we got into the car and drove off. Greatly fearing for our safety, they prayed for us. The next day, however, when Israel had conquered most of Jerusalem, her armies stationed at Rockefeller Museum fired across Jehoshephat Valley up to the Mount of Olives where the Jordanian armies were returning fire. The church was veiled in a cloud of fire and smoke. Our friends' fear turned to praise because they knew that wherever we were, we were as safe as we would have been in that fearful crossfire.

In Bethlehem four families, the elderly mother of Brother Kuttab, Kevin, and I took refuge in the Church of God. The building was big enough to house us all comfortably. Everyone had brought groceries, not foreseeing that the electricity would be cut off and we would have no way of storing perishables. Consequently, during the six days of war we literally feasted, lest the abundant supply of meat spoil.

The many children in our group knew nothing of the dangers around us for the first three days. They thought it was a big party. In an effort to protect them from fear, I gathered them into an interior room during the bombing raids for what I called a playtime. We sang our loudest action songs and played our noisiest games to drown out the roar of the bombers and the crash of the falling bombs. Of course, the children were delighted to be led by an adult in rowdy games that usually merited rebuke from their elders. No wonder they thought it was a party.

In the cellar under the church, scores of Bethlehemites crowded inside in anguished, screaming vigil. The adults had abandoned every effort of composure, and the terrified children, clawing at their distraught elders in a wild fight for self-preservation, contrasted with our happy, safe, carefree children. Many times I visited the cellar hoping to calm the adults and reassure the children. Having no personal experience with God and no living faith, they could not grasp my motive or my message. The only thing they could possibly imagine about my composure was that I simply had to be a collaborator with the Jews. Why else would I be so apparently indifferent to the advancing Israeli armies? They, who had had no time for God when they were in safety, had cut their connections to His comforting voice in the hour of danger. They were almost totally out of my reach.

Mubarak Awad, Brother Kuttab's nephew, was one of the most outstanding of all the young men in Bethlehem. While most young men hid themselves from dangers, Moby, as we called him, took my car and patrolled the streets of Bethlehem to rescue the wounded and take them to the hospital. Many died, but God spared Moby even in his exposure. While many cars were destroyed in their garages, my little ambulance received not a scratch.

On the third day of the war when Bethlehem capitulated, the bombing raids were increased and more wounded people came to seek first aid from our center. No longer could I hide the facts from our children who began to have interrogatory expressions. Taking them back into our playroom, I said, "Do you know what is going on out there? The grownups are angry with each other, and they are fighting like you children do sometimes. You know how you sometimes throw things or scratch each other or make each other bleed? Well, when grownups get into a country-wide free-for-all, they are worse than children. They throw bombs and break down whole buildings. Many people get hurt and some are killed. It is sad and dangerous, but we know we are children of God. He will protect us.

"Now let's play a different type of game," I suggested. "Who can tell me the story of someone in the Bible whom God protected in the middle of great danger?"

The children took turns giving detailed accounts of David, the three Hebrew children, Daniel, Peter, Paul and others. Finally, one child wanted to tell the story of Jonah. The story of Jonah seemed to be irrelevant at first, but there was a witness of the Spirit that God had a special message for us in Jonah's story.

"Children, do you know what Jonah prayed down in the belly of the whale?" I asked.

Seeing that they were interested, we all took Bibles and opened to the second chapter of Jonah. While we read the prayer, verses eight and nine gripped my attention. "They that observe lying vanities forsake their own mercy...Salvation is of the Lord."

Throughout the day those words kept returning to me. "Are you trying to tell me something, God?" I prayed. "I can't understand what you want me to know."

At 2 o'clock in the afternoon, jeeps went around Bethlehem announcing, "Flee from Bethlehem. In two hours the town will be razed!"

Mrs. Awad ran the mile or more from the hospital where she was working. "Take the children and flee to the desert!" she cried. "They are going to raze Bethlehem."

Forcefully, Jonah's prayer pounded in my temples. As rhythmically as my heartbeat a voice repeated, "Heed! Heed! Heed! Heed!"

Noticing my unperturbed silence, Mrs. Awad asked, "What are you going to do, Margaret?"

"God has already revealed His truth to me and I know

what I'll do," I affirmed. Then, I recounted the story of Jonah's prayer and my assurance that God had a message in it for us. "If you want to flee, don't walk. Take my car with some blankets, food and water. God keep you and the children. As for me God's presence is in this place. I'll stay here...'Salvation is of the Lord.'"

My attitude and the story perplexed them. They decided to pray. After the prayer peace filled their spirits and they decided to stay. For some reason the threat to raze Bethlehem was not executed. Praise God! He spared the children and us a miserable night in the cold desert.

Not everyone was spared. Thousands of terrified adults wearing expressions of utter despair passed under our balcony in a silent half-trot. Carrying hastily wrapped bundles, they dragged weary, terror-stricken children whose short legs could scarcely keep pace but whose quickened imagination drove them onward from the unknown devourer that pursued them. Had they only known the Lord!

Ironically, with the end of the war came the end of our feasting. All the roads were closed to civilian travel. Trucks could not transport produce to the city markets. For weeks all that was available in the Bethlehem market were grape leaves, marrows which were cultivated in family gardens around Bethlehem, and the white and black types of mulberries from trees growing all over the city.

Communications between East Jerusalem, the West Bank and the outside world were interrupted. It was six weeks before mail from the United States reached me. The first news from my family informed me that my father had terminal cancer and had less than three months to live. He wanted to see me. To have gone to him would have compromised my rights to return to my mission station. The agonizing battle of loyalties would continue to tear at me until September 14, when my father would be released from his suffering without my having been privileged to return to his side.

Three weeks after the war was over, under military escort I was allowed to return to Jerusalem to assess the damages to the church on the Mount of Olives. Three bombs had hit the church. Two had opened wide holes in the stone walls. A third had ripped out the iron window frame, twisted it up like a corkscrew, and stabbed it right through the pulpit. The songbooks and Bibles were scattered all over the floor and buried under the debris of the splintered benches and the fallen plaster that had been riddled by small arms fire. The apartment adjoining the church was also heavily damaged. It would have been most unlikely that anyone would have escaped death had they stayed there during the battle. Thank God I had been spared.

Standing in the ravaged church, the Israeli officer said, "I'm so sorry. This really should never happen, especially to churches, hospitals and schools." Although I could foresee the burden and expense of repairing the building, I rejoiced with the conviction that it was a sign that the Gentile Age is ending. We shall not need a church many more years.

Six weeks after the war ended, I was permitted to return to Jerusalem, but I could not move my furniture back. The electricity and water had not been reconnected. A 24-inch bomb lay unexploded just outside my door, attracting the interest of all the neighborhood children. Long months of rehabilitation lay ahead. There were no energizing charges of adrenaline to sustain me for the challenge, but the hymn "Be Still My Soul" emerged from my subconscious to steer me through the months ahead.

The days followed each other in monotonous similarity. Rising before dawn, I finished the chores at home and joined thousands of others who trudged daily across the debris of ruined buildings to stand in interminable lines at registration centers. The car had to be registered at the traffic department. The church property had to be registered at the land registry office. My identity card had to be changed from Jordanian to Israeli. My driver's license had to be changed. Only a limited number of people could hope to complete the formalities each day. Thousands were standing by three in the morning hoping that they would be served before the offices closed at 2 o'clock in the afternoon. From 5 o'clock every evening there was curfew.

For six weeks I stood in those lines all day every day, and it was not until November that I had completed all the formalities. It is impossible to explain how wearisome it was to stand for long hours, exposed to the hot summer sun. I took with me a bottle of lukewarm water to appease my thirst and some books to read. I often knitted. Waiting was not an enjoyable experience.

Finally, I obtained a special military travel permit to go to Aboud village where I had started a church in 1964. The war had scarcely touched the village, and everyone was fine. They made the most of daylight hours to harvest their grain and care for their vineyards. Curfew at 5 o'clock shortened their workday and increased my opportunity to visit them at night.

This visitation period was brief because the military commander of our district sent officers to arrest me, charging that I was a spy. I never did learn whether I was being accused of spying for the Arabs or for the Jews. The commander interrogated me for two hours. Unconvinced that I was a spy, he released me with the order to appear before a higher official in Ramallah the following day for interrogation. When that second officer cross-examined me for two hours, he was convinced that I was not a spy. Not only did he free me, he also gave me special permission to visit the villagers after curfew. The whole episode was a trial to my overtaxed body and spirit, but it gave me unique opportunities to witness of my Savior and present His gospel to men of important status.

Since I could not move my furniture back from

Bethlehem, I slept with Kevin on the hard tile floor. Even with rising before dawn, the night was long. I would go to bed before 8 o'clock to avoid wasting my meager supply of candles. What a lonely vigil! At night the silence seem to scream hauntingly that my father was grieving because I had not come to his bedside. My sunburned face ached. My muscles complained. "Be Still My Soul" pushed its way through my clamorous thoughts and lulled me off to sleep.

Nearly every day Kevin would escape from me in the afternoon. I could not find him, and after curfew I would wait, hoping he would return safely. When he returned, I tried to reason with him.

"Kevin," I said, "you are a beautiful, valuable dog. How would I ever explain to Elizabeth if you were killed or stolen? You just can't keep running away and worrying me like this."

It seemed that Kevin tried to understand and that he wanted to obey, but he kept running away. Finally, I could no longer cope. The next time he ran away, I whipped him. The poor dog's eyes reflected his shock. Kevin went into an empty room, turned his face to the wall and softly whined out his despair. I sensed that there must be a reason for Kevin's behavior. We had braved many weeks of very trying circumstances together. Kevin's grief was more painful to me than his escapades had been. He was my friend.

"Kevin," I called. "Come get your food." Nothing doing. He would neither eat nor drink. His unbroken, soft whining crushed me.

"Kevin," I begged, "come sleep where you always do." There was no move, no response.

"All right, then, Kevin, I'll move in and sleep beside you," I said, looking deeply into his eyes. There I saw despair, a sort of hopeless relinquishment. I could not bear it. Suddenly, I understood his problem.

God had inscribed a law in that poor dog's instinct that he must protect his mistress. To make matters more complex, his mistress had instructed him to obey me until she returned. With the odor of blood and death all about us, Kevin was driven to search out and find Elizabeth. Was he trying to obey me? He had his own bewildering battle of loyalties with less reasoning power to aid him in coping. When I punished him for performing his God-given duty, Kevin was overwhelmed.

Feeling sorry for myself and ashamed of my impatience born of misunderstanding, I threw my arms around his neck and cried, " Forgive me, Kevin. I'm so sorry I misunderstood. I should have known. I, too, am supposed to be loyal to my dying father as well as loyal to my distressed disciples. I'm almost to the point of despair like you, Kevin. We're just two dogs, you and I. Kevin, do forgive me." Clinging to the dog while the darkness closed in on us, I wept.

Did my weakness manifested in my abundant tears stimulate Kevin to overcome his despair? I do not know. With magnanimity he accepted me the next day. I promised him I would take him daily to look for Elizabeth, which promise I kept until she returned. He would almost drag me in his haste to go where Elizabeth had the apartment. Not finding her there, he would look at me sadly. When I told him, "Kevin, she is fine. She will come back soon," he would believe me and be happy again.

After three months I finally obtained permission to move my furniture back from Bethlehem. Elizabeth had returned by then, and she worked with me all day to get everything back in order. About five in the evening, to relax, Elizabeth and I drove to Ramallah. I wanted to buy some aisle carpets for the church, but the shop was closed. I returned without stopping the car. Curfew had been changed to 7 o'clock, so I had time to eat supper with Elizabeth and Margaret before I returned home.

As I lay in my own bed for the first time in three months, I praised God for keeping me through the extremely stressful situations of the past months. There were still problems. My father was still suffering. The church still needed repairs. I had water but no electricity. Nevertheless, I was encouraged. Somehow, with Elizabeth and Margaret back I felt less alone. I expected to emerge soon from the entire nightmare.

The following day two distinguished gentlemen came to my house. Assuming them to be representatives of the Israeli government who had come to verify my report of war damages on the church, I invited them to come in. As soon as they were seated, they began to interrogate me.

"Where were you yesterday?" the officer asked.

"I was here all day. My furniture was moved back from Bethlehem, and I spent the day arranging it," I answered.

"Did you go out in the evening?" he continued.

"At five o'clock in the evening I drove to Ramallah and right back. I was back by five-thirty," I replied.

"Did you drive past the American Colony?" he asked.

"No, I went and returned by Mount Scopus," I assured him. "But why are you asking me all these questions?"

"Miss Gaines," he spoke firmly, "a brown-haired lady driving a light blue Volkswagen with your license plate number ran over a child near the American Colony shortly after five o'clock yesterday afternoon and fled from the scene of the accident. We are charging you with the crime and have come to arrest you."

Stunned by the incredible words I was hearing, I closed my eyes and waited. Never in my life had I had an accident. How could I prove my innocence? How many more distressing situations was I going to face to knock me back into my interminable nightmare? Then "Be Still My Soul" crashed through my gloom and lifted my spirits.

Opening my eyes, I smiled and said, "Gentlemen, it is fantastic the way God prepares us for life's enigmas and vicissitudes and how He returns again and again to lead us through it all. Before the war God gave me a hymn that has steadied me through the conflict, through the dreadful rehabilitation, through the terminal illness of my father and my frustrated desires to see him before he dies, and through my arrest on the alleged charges that I was a spy. Now, it is that hymn that returns to guide me through this new incredible test. I know nothing of this accusation, but if you have time and will let me share the hymn with you, you will see the secret of my composure." While the chief of Jerusalem's police force and his deputy listened intently, I recited the entire hymn. Before I had finished, we all three were yielding to the flow of tears.

"I do not believe you are guilty," said the chief. "Don't you know anyone who can verify your story?"

"Yes, Elizabeth Van Heamstra was with me all day yesterday and even went with me to Ramallah. Would you like to see her?" I asked.

"Yes, indeed," he answered. "Come show me to her house."

After interrogating Elizabeth, they were satisfied that my alibi was valid, so they did not arrest me. However, the wonderful opportunity I had to witness to the absolute goodness of my Lord justified the distressing experience that provided it.

For many weeks I tried to get permission for Mousa Issa Saleh, a young man from our church in Aboud, to go to our Bible school in Switzerland. He could not leave the country without signing that he would never return. We hoped to get permission for him to study abroad and return. Waiting to see the military governor about this business, I was spied by the officer who had interrogated me. He was in the governor's office, and he told the governor about me. I was called to his office.

Again, I was interrogated for two hours. Finally, the governor said, "Miss Gaines, do you really believe that wicked men like the captain and me are chosen people of God?"

"You asked me a question," I replied. "Will you permit me to answer it?"

"Yes, take your liberty. I am listening," he said.

"You said 'wicked men, like the captain and me.' If you really feel that you are wicked and have tried repeatedly to keep God's law and failed, there is hope for you. Have you heard of the laws of the leper?" I asked.

"Yes, I studied all that before my bar mitzvah," he replied.

"Then you know that a confirmed leper was exiled from his home and community. Did you also know," I asked, "that a leper completely covered with leprosy and hopelessly defiled by the disease could go to the priest? After showing him his condition and confessing that he was a hopeless leper, the priest could pronounce him clean?"

"What! Is that in the Torah?" he exclaimed.

"Yes, you will find it in Leviticus 13:12, 13," I said. "Imagine the mercy of God in this law. Since leprosy typifies sin, would not a hopeless sinner find cleansing mercy if he shows himself to God, confesses his condition, and asks for mercy?

"Also, you said, 'Do you think we are chosen people of God?' I affirm that I believe the Scriptures say that Jehovah chose Israel as a bride. It is marvelous to be chosen. But Jehovah also required that a bride-elect choose to be the wife of the groom before a marriage could be legally consummated. Yes, Jehovah has chosen you and the captain. Have you chosen Him?"

Then and now my objective is to point leprous people to the cleansing fountain that flows from Immanuel's veins.

Slowly, the West Bank Arabs adjusted to the occupation. They did not need me as much as when the war first ended. The Missions Board requested that I return to the United States for a furlough.

"Lord," I prayed, "I hate to leave the people at this time. If it is your will for me to go, please let me return with the money to build a church in Aboud. I promise to give everything that I receive as gifts or offerings for this purpose."

With that secret hope in my mind, I left Israel on July 16, 1968, for a much-needed rest in America.

Chapter 13

⁕

GET UP AND GET AT IT

Aboud is situated 33 miles northwest of Jerusalem. A prominent place in the time of Christ, it has since declined to a simple village of 3,000 population. Ruins of seven Byzantine churches which served its bustling 40,000 inhabitants in the fifth century stand as silent reminders that Aboud was an early Christian stronghold. The Moslem population, which was only 100 in 1873, has since increased to half the total population of the village.

For centuries Aboud's people were simple peasants, living mainly from their olive and almond trees and cultivating small kitchen gardens. The young families migrated to the cities to find employment and better educational opportunities for their children until Israel, needing manpower, provided transportation for the villagers and employed them in her factories, citrus groves and in construction. Consequently, many new families have remained in Aboud since 1967, enhancing the life of the village.

Invariably, visitors ask me how I found Aboud. My own story is linked to an Anglican missionary who served Aboud for 16 consecutive years before World War I. Miss Nicholson was the last Protestant missionary to Aboud. Although she did not return to Aboud after 1914, her influence lives on. Her students, having long since become senior citizens, still recite the psalms and sing the songs she taught them.

The Saleh family associated more with Miss Nicholson than anyone else. Ibrahim Saleh, who was a teacher in the school she founded, lived to bless our congregation until July 1972, when he died at the age of 115 years.

The Khalil Saleh family were God's agents in helping us have a congregation in Aboud. Khalil Saleh had a beautiful daughter named Zarefie, who lost her sight when she was 5 years old. Her father placed her in a Lutheran boarding school where she learned to love Jesus. At her confirmation, she really gave her heart to the Lord. Through the years she became acquainted with many Christian leaders, including Brother Kuttab.

Zarefie taught school in the city for a number of years. When her aged parents needed her help, she returned to Aboud, where she had no spiritual fellowship except with Ibrahim Saleh and his sister-in-law, Azizi. Longing for companionship and the rekindling of the gospel fires in Aboud, Zarefie prayed daily for God to send a missionary to her village.

In May 1964 Brother Kuttab asked me, "Would you like to visit a truly beautiful Arab village? We should like for you to meet our friend, Zarefie."

"Yes, I would love to. When may we go?" I answered.

"As soon as you would like. Why not now?" he replied. So we drove to Aboud.

Aboud has more olive trees than any village I know. Snuggled in the heart of the olive groves, Aboud is a gem of old stone houses. Most of them are from the Turkish occupation era, but some of them date back to the time of Christ.

Immediately, my heart embraced the village. The hospitality as well as its aesthetic beauty won me.

Sitting in Khalil Saleh's humble house, I recognized taboon bread on the tray which Zarefie's sister carried to the room. Taboon bread is still baked on live coals as Gideon baked it for the angel.

"Oh, that is taboon bread, isn't it?" I blurted out. "I haven't eaten any since I was in Tunisia."

Immediately, they brought me a low table and served me hot taboon bread, olives, oil and onion. I devoured the delicious bread with gusto to the surprise of Brother Kuttab. Mrs. Kuttab, an excellent cook, had prepared every kind of delicious food for me, but I could not really enjoy it because of my exhaustion from my trip from France. This plain bread suited me better than anything I had eaten.

My love for Aboud was reciprocated. Zarefie invited me to come and conduct services in her father's home. I agreed and the very next week began the services that resulted in the founding of the Church of God in Aboud.

For 16 months I traveled to Aboud once a week for a children's Bible lesson and an adult worship service. Then in September 1965 I rented a small apartment and began to live in Aboud from Thursday through Saturday each week.

When I first started going to Aboud, I also started going once a week to Amman, the capital city of Jordan. When I rented the apartment in Aboud, I also rented an apartment in Amman so I could care for the new church I founded there. Three days in Aboud and four days in Amman, I carried on a full church program for both congregations.

While I was on furlough in 1968, I did not divulge to anyone my plan to build a church in Aboud, but never before have I ever received offerings to equal what I received on that trip. True to my promise, I kept every cent for the construction of the building. When I returned I had $3,000 and the bonus which the World Missions Board gave me for returning early to the field.

Using the physical building for an object lesson, I taught the young church what the spiritual counterparts are: the foundation, the stones, the chief cornerstone, and the cement that holds it all together.

On September 13, 1969, our lovely little church was dedicated. Friends from all over Israel and the West Bank came to share our joy. The stone edifice, its garden wall, its furniture and an electric generator had cost a total of $10,000, and all was fully paid before the dedication. How we praised God for His gift to Aboud!

While I rejoiced over the finished building, I secretly hoped I would never build so much as a chicken coop again. It had been an extremely trying summer for me.

Brother Kuttab had moved his family to the United States in the winter of 1968. The Rev. and Mrs. Milton Hay were sent to replace Brother Kuttab. Brother Hay supervised the Middle East Theological Institute competently, and he enjoyed tremendous influence with the young men whom he served untiringly. I continued to teach at the Institute and manage its cafeteria and housekeeping chores, along with my pastoral duties in Aboud. Simultaneously, I was national and local secretary and treasurer. I kept four sets of financial books and maintained a heavy load of correspondence.

Understandably, Brother Hay refused to be involved in

the building program which had not been initiated through the regular procedures of the organization. I had no right to implicate him in my scheme. The most lonely experience I had ever known (even though I had no one to blame for it) was to have an overseer with whom I could not confer.

The exhausting duties combined with acute mucous colitis depleted my resistance and resulted in my spending three months in the hospital in 1969.

While I was in the hospital, my doctor wisely confronted me. "Miss Gaines," he began, "you are surely going to die. You are not digesting food. Your blood is dangerously low. We have tried every known treatment with no response. You are pleasant and communicative, but you are inert. You seem to be totally indifferent as to whether or not you get well." Continuing he said, "Unless you deliberately care for yourself and try to cooperate with the treatment, there is no hope for you. What a waste! You could get well and live a long productive life. Why don't you think that over?"

With these startling remarks, which seemingly squarely placed on me the responsibility for my living or dying, he left the room.

All night I pondered what the doctor had said, and I had to agree with him. I was not depressed. Total exhaustion hindered me from concentrating on my responsibility, and I had really left the problem of my living or dying in the hands of my doctor and my God. To be confronted with personal responsibility troubled me.

"God, is it true what the doctor says? Am I totally indifferent to whether I live or die? My life has been rich and full. It would not seem a pity to die even at my age. But it isn't fair to you, God, for me to lie down and die. You have put up with me through the years, delivering me from numerous psychological complexes. You patiently led me through my adjustments and helped me learn the languages I needed. Only now are you getting me to a state where I can be useful to you. I must be willing, even eager, to give you my healthy body for your purpose now. But in my weakness, I cannot react. I am willing to cooperate deliberately with the treatment provided. Strengthen my will and deliver me from the inertia. The power ultimately is yours."

God did deliver me from my inertia. Although it took a full year, I recovered to undertake the greatest challenge of my life. The new challenge came soon after I left the hospital.

The people in Aboud, from the time I first entered the village, begged me to begin an elementary school for girls. Public schools are not coeducational in Jordan. In Aboud the only government school was for boys. There was a Catholic school for girls, but its religious restrictions made it difficult for non-Catholics.

In our 1969 budget request, Brother Hay proposed beginning an elementary school. When the new budget was approved, it provided for an elementary school with $150 a month for operational expense.

No one was more surprised than I that the Church of God approved the proposition. Still struggling to recover my health, I ignored the school project until February 1970. The $150 had arrived regularly since September 1969 for the non-existent school, and I could ignore it no longer. I decided to pray through.

"God, everyone seems to want an elementary school, but I do not want the responsibility of it. I already have more responsibility than I can handle. Besides, I know nothing about elementary education. I have no training, and I'm not physically able to cope. It must be only man that wants the school. You do not want it, do you God?" I argued.

"Get up and get at it!" He challenged.

"God, I don't understand your purpose, but I yield my mind and my body to you. I'm willing to read and study, but spare me from wasting time on useless books. I'm willing to listen to instruction and the advice of competent educators, but do please protect me from the confusing concepts of the inept. Knowing your will, my Lord, I delight to do it."

First, I drew plans for school desks, benches and chalkboards. A carpenter in the neighboring village, Bir Zeit, agreed to make the furniture for $1,500 and to have it completed by August.

There was no place to house the school. The landlady, who had rented us a room for our church services in 1965 when the congregation outgrew Zarefie's father's house, was struggling to build a second floor to her house. Secretly, I wrote a letter to her husband, a prosperous businessman in Venezuela, asking him to please send his wife the necessary money to finish her new apartment. I told him of my desire to rent the entire lower floor of her house in order to start a school. Immediately, he complied. The new apartment was completed by midsummer, giving me a place to put the school furniture and organize our facilities in time for the 1970-71 term.

A school is more than a well-furnished building. What about the license to open the school? What about teachers and a curriculum?

In March I made application to the director of education of the Ramallah District. Friends told me that it could take months, even years to obtain a license. To my utter astonishment, my application was approved within six weeks.

During the summer I interviewed a number of prospective teachers from Aboud. I hired four. They had no teacher training, only a high school diploma and a special government certificate. Their salaries would be very low.

I knew I would have to study education myself in order to teach the teachers. Initially, the school was destined to be an inservice training center for all of us.

Investigating textbooks printed by the Ministry of Education, I found them sadly inadequate and, for some classes, non-existent. It was imperative that I initiate a curriculum of study and plan worksheets for the classes. There were no textbooks. By the end of the summer, I had drawn thousands of pictures and duplicated much material with which to begin the year.

With the physical plant, teachers and study materials provided, I turned my attention to the duties of headmistress. "Oh, God, I don't know what is expected of me," I prayed. "Do please teach me." How marvelously that prayer was answered.

In the best bookstore in Jerusalem I looked for some books to guide principals of elementary schools. To my amazement, I found a compact but complete booklet for school inspectors—*What To Look For When Inspecting Schools.* Wonderful! I had not thought of that! It was like finding a copy of a test. All I had to do was learn the answers. If I knew what inspectors were expecting to find, I would know precisely what I had to do.

Besides the safety and sanitary conditions of the school building and playgrounds, the booklet discussed the proper scheduling of departmentalized systems. It pointed out the necessity of posting a complete school schedule on the main information board, as well as having the schedule for each class posted in the classrooms. Individual teacher schedules had to be posted on the main information board. All this information had to be in permanent files.

In addition to the schedule of studies, a table of school

census had to be displayed on the main information board. The total number of boys and girls, and the total number of students for each class had to be stipulated on the census record. Proper attendance records had to be kept, and the required number of school days for the nine-month term carefully fulfilled. A permanent record with required information on each student had to be on file.

It was the duty of the headmistress to inspect teachers periodically and to keep a permanent file of their class-room performance records. This included inspecting their annual teaching scheme, their daily lesson plans, and their ability to test the students according to the behavioral objectives. Monthly teachers' meetings provided opportunities to advise the faculty of progressive information from the board of education and to coordinate local activities with the district. Records of the teachers' meetings and the minutes had to be permanently filed.

All this and other vital information was presented in the booklet. With all my objectives clearly spelled out, I could advance without wasting time.

First, I made the schedule for our departmentalized school, planned the files for our permanent records, and prepared forms for pertinent information on faculty, students and every phase of our program and planning. Fortunately, inspectors do not visit a new school until the second term. It took several terms of school for me to reach my own initial objectives.

In August 1970 as the date for our official opening approached, I was so tense that my wristwatch would not tolerate my magnetism. When I tried to wear the watch, the hands would spin erratically and then stop. Although my general health had improved while I was totally absorbed by the intense preparations for our school, I felt like I was on a runaway treadmill. How could I ever cope with a school when just preparations for its opening overwhelmed me? God would simply have to calm me, so I decided to pray through about it.

Kneeling early one morning in late August, I purposed to spend as much time in prayer as I needed in order to obtain peace and calm.

"Look at me, God!" I exclaimed. "As tense as I am, you cannot trust me in a school. I haven't a single teacher yet nor a student and I could just explode. How can I coordinate school activities and guide teacher relationships among themselves, with me and with the students? I'll destroy everything in the outset unless you help me."

With my need concisely expressed, I could pray no more. I could only wait and listen. For several years I had longed to find the words to an old hymn I remembered my mother singing. I did not know the title of the hymn, nor did I know the first line. My efforts to find the hymn had failed until that moment when I waited, listening for some word from God. Opening an old Methodist hymnal, my eyes fell upon the following words written by John Greenleaf Whittier:

> Dear Lord and Father of mankind,
>
> Forgive our fev'rish ways;
>
> Reclothe us in our rightful mind,
>
> In purer lives thy service find,
>
> In deeper reverence, praise.
>
>
> In simple trust like theirs who heard,
>
> Beside the Syrian sea,
>
> The gracious calling of the Lord,
>
> Let us, like them, without a word,
>
> Rise up and follow Thee.

Get Up And Get At It

O sabbath, rest of Galilee,

O calm of hills above,

Where Jesus knelt to share with Thee

The silence of eternity,

Interpreted by love!

Drop Thy still dews of quietness,

Till all my strivings cease;

Take from our souls the strain and stress,

And let our ordered lives confess

The beauty of Thy peace.

Phrase by phrase I prayed the timely hymn. *"Oh, Lord, forgive our fev'rish ways.* That's it, God," I cried. "I told you I am tense from all my feverish activities. There is nothing in all the Scriptures that portrays you as upset or out of control. This can't be right. I have to lack faith or understanding or both to be in this state. *Reclothe us in our rightful mind*...exactly, Lord," I continued. "There is nothing in my feverishness that is indicative of your beautiful, calm sanity. Anything short of your calm has to be some degree of insanity. Do restore me to my rightful mind. Then perceiving you I shall have more reverence. Having more reverence, I'll have more purity of service and praise.

"In simple trust like theirs who heard, beside the Syrian sea, the gracious calling of the Lord, let us, like them, without a word, rise up and follow thee. I hear you calling me to you, to your perfect rest. Give me simplicity of trust so that I, like the disciples who left their ships and nets without a discussion, may also rise up and enter your peace. Too many protests clamor in my mind, Lord. Rectify my focus

177

on your face. Intensify my perception of your person. Only then shall the clamor of human reasoning be silenced. Only then, caught up in the wonder of what you are, will I rise to your calling.

"O sabbath, rest of Galilee, O calm of hills above, where Jesus knelt to share with Thee, the silence of eternity interpreted by love. Yes, Father. Bring me also into communion with your love so concentrated as to still all motion and hush all sound in its tangible silent expression.

"Drop Thy still dews of quietness; till all my strivings cease. Do Lord," I prayed. "All my strivings cannot produce a success, whether it be a school, a church, a life. My noisy activities can only destroy. Drop Thy healing dews to quiet my spirit. Calm my striving. Hold me still, Lord, until I relax and relinquish everything to you.

"Take from our souls the strain and stress and let our ordered lives confess, the beauty of Thy peace. Master, order my life by your perfect designs and to your rhythm. Therein is real beauty. Thereby is peace."

All day I prayed the hymn. By sunset I had entered into His calm. His love covered me. There was no further need for words. What I expected to be a temporary grace proved to be an abiding state of rest in the Lord which has only rarely been threatened.

The Aboud Elementary School began on schedule. The abiding peace of the Lord graced our activities and His wisdom guided our paths. He met our daily needs, but totally unexpected circumstances further tested my new-found rest.

While visiting with Mrs. Milton Hay the following spring, she surprised me by announcing, "Margaret, I have to tell you that our family is leaving the mission field. You will be alone to assume all the responsibilities, so it is only fair that I delay no longer breaking the news."

"When do you expect to leave?" I asked in semi-shock.

"I shall be leaving with my three girls within two weeks," she hastily replied. "My husband will leave later after he settles all his business."

She left as planned, and Brother Hay followed her in the late summer. I had been totally unaware that anything threatened to curtail their missionary tenure, but our national church did not believe my ignorance. Everyone in Jerusalem and Bethlehem blamed me for Brother Hay's departure. Their inevitable reaction exploded against me in a fierce verbal assault. The young men held Brother Hay in the highest esteem. They simply could not accept his departure.

The peace of God sustained me while ministering to those who were outright rejecting me and blaming me for what they could not understand. In varying degrees I had to cope with this relentless rebellion for 16 months until the arrival of Walter Greiner and his dear wife, Elfrieda. Yes, she was the same Elfrieda who had dedicated her life to missions when I went to Germany in 1958. She had since married Walter Greiner, and they had three lovely girls and a fine son. Their arrival in Israel brought unspeakable comfort to me.

By the end of our first term of school, I faced a new decision. The apartment where the school began had four rooms, a kitchen and an entrance hall. At best it would be adequate for only two years. There was no bigger place to rent in Aboud. Not knowing what to do, but knowing I could not just wait and see, I determined to seek God about it.

"Lord, we shall have outgrown our premises by this time next year. Are you going to work this problem out without me? Is there something I need to do?" I earnestly prayed.

"On the Shukba Road there is a plot of land. Buy it and build a school," came the reply.

Build a school! I who did not want to build so much as a chicken coop was being challenged to build a school! Yes, but ultimately my mind and body were only instruments which God used. He accepted His own challenge through me and the results were marvelous.

Chapter 14

❧

As God Provides

On Shukba Road there was only one plot of land which was barren of trees and fit my vision of the lot God indicated I should buy. For some reason the owner, an elderly man whose sons were all out of the country, refused emphatically to sell. He referred me to the lot adjoining his land. It was for sale, so I purchased it and prepared to build.

Realizing it was absurd to build inadequate facilities, I planned the building large enough to accommodate the upper and lower kindergarten classes, the first through sixth elementary classes, and other rooms relevant to the school's activities. I took the plans to the architect who drew the blueprints from them.

I went to the best contractor in the Ramallah district to get an estimate of construction costs. I did not know this contractor, but he was highly recommended to me.

When I returned to the contractor after three days, he told me that he estimated the building would cost $42,000. Drawing a deep breath, I prepared to make him an unreasonable proposition.

"I feel like I must proceed with plans to build this school in Aboud," I began. "It will be constructed in the name of the Church of God, but it must be clearly stipulated that the Church of God is not responsible for this contract. I alone am responsible. All I have is $2,800 which I would give to you on the signing of the contract. Since I have no collateral, the balance of the cost I shall pay as God provides. I realize that humanly speaking, I am literally asking you to build Aboud a school and let God pay you when and how He will. Therefore, if you refuse, I shall not blame you, but if you choose to enter this venture of faith with me, we shall see how God plans to honor the contract. What do you think about it?"

"I shall accept the contract," he agreed. Thereupon, the contract was immediately written up, including the terms of my paying "as God provides." It was then signed by the contractor and me and duly witnessed. This was an amazing agreement on the contractor's part, considering that he did not know me from Adam.

Torrential rain hampered my drive back to Aboud that night. Struggling to see while I drove, I was conscious of an amusing unreality that teased my mind. "Did I really sign a contract for $42,000? Either God is planning something marvelous or I'm the biggest fool I've ever met." A peaceful assurance inspired me to get set to stand still and see God work.

Two weeks after the signing of the contract, there was a surprise devaluation of the Israeli currency that would have greatly diminished the value of the $2,800, besides doubling construction costs within three months. The experienced contractor began preparing the construction materials. He ordered the stone and hired the stonecutters to shape them for the mason. The actual construction would begin after the rainy season.

In February 1972 Dr. J. Herbert Walker, Jr., the Church of God overseer of Europe and the Middle East, visited the Holy Land. When he came to Aboud, I told him, "I'm so glad you are here. I want to tell you what we plan to do. Today, you will preside over the groundbreaking ceremonies for the new school we plan to build."

"How far are you along with your plans?" he inquired.

"The contract is signed and the contractor is preparing to begin the building as soon as the rainy season is over," I answered.

"What type of building are you planning, and what are the estimated costs?" he asked.

"I'll show you the blueprint. The costs are estimated at $42,000," I answered.

After a deep sigh, Dr. Walker advised, "Don't look back, Sister Margaret." Then he asked me, "When did you sign this contract?"

"I haven't paid much attention to the exact date," I replied. "I'll get my copy of the contract, and we shall see."

Getting my contract I looked at the date and suddenly found it to be significant. The contract was signed on December 6, 1971. That was 25 years to the hour from December 6, 1946, when I received my mission call. Was it a coincidence that the signing of the contract honored the date of my mission call? I think God deliberately witnessed that He approved my call and the contract.

How little I realized the impact of my business management. What a predicament I must have put Dr. Walker into. Only later did I appreciate his greatness of spirit in managing the situation.

The following day Dr. Walker led the congregation in the groundbreaking ceremonies. There was nowhere to look but forward. There was no turning back.

Headmistress duties and pastoral duties absorbed all my attention the following weeks. The construction continued without my having to be concerned with it. The contractor was the old-fashioned type of honorable man who valued his word and a job well done above his very life. He reminded me of my father.

During the Passover week, the Rev. W.E. Johnson, general director of World Missions, stopped by Israel on his return trip from South Africa. No hotel rooms were available, so Brother Johnson had to stay in Aboud.

The day after Brother Johnson's arrival, the contractor came and interrupted our discussion.

"Sister, tomorrow we shall start pouring the foundation. Is it not your custom to have a religious ceremony for the occasion?" he asked.

What wonderful timing! "Yes, I want to introduce you to the general director of World Missions. He is here to perform the offices," I answered. "When will you start?"

"My men will have everything prepared by 8 o'clock in the morning, if that isn't too early," he replied.

"That is fine," I assured him.

"What is the trouble, Sister Margaret?" asked Brother Johnson. He had not understood the conversation as it had all been in the Arabic language.

"Nothing is wrong," I assured him. "You have just arrived in time to perform the offices for the foundation-pouring ceremonies of our new school building," I informed him. "The contractor said they will be prepared for us at 8 o'clock tomorrow morning."

The following morning I prepared a New Testament,

symbol of Christ the Word of God made flesh and a small bottle of olive oil and salt, both symbols of the Holy Spirit. These we laid carefully in the foundation during the ceremony which Brother Johnson conducted so beautifully. Then he honored us by shoveling the first cement into the foundation. The elders of the Aboud church followed his example. Finally, each one of the congregation added cement before the benediction was pronounced, and the workers resumed their labor.

Brother Johnson noticed my extreme shortness of breath. He warned me to be careful lest I suffer a heart attack. He insisted that I return to the United States during the summer for a furlough.

Immediately following the closing of the school term in June 1972, I left Aboud for two months in America. It was an emotional trip for me. Since my 1968 visit, there were a number of new family graves to visit. My youngest sister, Ollie, had died at the age of 42. My brother's mother-in-law, his wife and his son (age 23) had all followed closely behind my father and my uncle. My family was scattered, so everywhere I traveled the wounds of mourning were re-opened.

In that frame of mind I was not inclined to solicit financial support for our construction project. Also, my project had not been officially approved by our World Missions Board.

While I was in Cleveland, Tennessee, during the camp meeting season. Brother W.E. Johnson officiated at the camp meeting Missions Day program. He requested that I greet the people briefly. He surprised me by saying: "I feel like telling them about your building and letting them give, if they so desire."

"Oh, no!" I exclaimed. "You must not do that. Go ahead and raise support for your approved budget."

After a short conversation about the approved budget,

Brother Johnson repeated, "Sister Margaret, I am sure God would have me to share with the Tennessee Camp Meeting what is going on in Aboud and let them have a part in your project."

"How can I question your guidance from the Lord?" I answered. "Still, I am not worried about the financing of the school building. What God orders He pays for as well. This is not an approved project. You are responsible to raise money for approved projects," I insisted.

For the remainder of our ride to the campground we indulged in light conversation, dropping the subject of Aboud.

Just before entering the tabernacle where the camp meeting crowd had assembled, Brother Johnson assured me he would obey God's leading for him and divulge my mission activities, however briefly. This he did. When the offering was taken later for various mission projects, pledges of over $7,000 were made for the new Aboud school. In the following months the pledges were fully paid, but totally unsolicited offerings, mostly in small amounts, constituted most of our total budget. The contractor witnessed the faithfulness of God to keep His contract.

The months following my return to Israel were so full that I could not take any interest in the construction pro–ject. My brother Paul, alone after the loss of his wife and son, had returned to Israel with me. A lady who met me on my arrival at the Tel Aviv Airport said she had come to stay indefinitely to help me in the mission work. She had lost her husband. Besides trying to get visas for my broth-er and that lady, I had to try to manage some suitable housing for them in my inadequate apartment and assist them in their adjustment.

The new term of school began shortly after my return. How thankful I was for a trustworthy contractor who needed no supervision.

Primitive living conditions quickly proved too much for my lady guest. After two months she returned to America. My brother stayed with me five months. When we received the news that Ollie's husband had terminal cancer, Paul returned to the United States. Within a year of her death Ollie's husband followed her.

My multitudinous duties in the home, office, church and school screamed for urgent attention after Paul's departure. For weeks I worked constantly to catch up. More and more I realized I simply had to have a dependable coworker.

For six years Arlene Miller, an elementary school teacher and evangelist from Ohio, had written to me. The Spirit of God kept impressing on me that Arlene was His chosen helper for me. Mary Lou Amburgy had met Arlene several times. She also suggested that Arlene could really help me in Aboud. In March 1973 I wrote to Arlene asking her if she would consider giving a year of volunteer work in Aboud.

God had already been preparing Arlene. She knew she would be a permanent full-time missionary. Quietly, she made her plans and was ready. She was only waiting for my invitation. She answered me that she would come in July. Overwhelmed with my work and physically exhausted from a prolonged bronchial congestion, I did not write Arlene another word, nor did I answer her inquiries for the following four months. Nevertheless, acting on my invitation and God's guidance, she determined to come as planned.

The contractor had hoped to have the building completed by November 1972. Because of various complications, mostly rising out of the devaluation of the Israeli currency and subsequent difficulties obtaining supplies and hiring workers, its completion was delayed until March 1973.

During our noon break from classes on March 25, 1973, the contractor came to the school. "Sister, the building is finally completed," he announced. "Would you come look it over? If you are pleased, I shall give you the keys today."

Together we went through the lovely building. Everything was in good order. The contractor gave me the keys. Unwittingly he had honored another significant date. On March 25, 1952, around noon, I had boarded the train in Anniston for my departure to Tunisia. For God it was no coincidence that the 21st anniversary of my departure for the mission field was thus marked. How deeply I felt the significance of the marking of two important events of my life by the construction of our school. Seemingly, God had literally given me the school building as an anniversary gift.

Did God honor His contract? Yes, indeed, He did. When the contractor handed me the keys to the building, he was paid in full.

In April it was imperative that we move into the new building. During physical education classes, the students leveled the playground carrying hills of dirt and stone. Invigorated by the joy of their spacious facilities, each child and faculty member participated in beautifying the campus. It kept everyone busy until the end of the term.

What a relief it was to me to complete the final examinations and turn in my reports to the director of education. The 18-to-22 hours a day work schedule of heavy responsibilities and strenuous physical work overtaxed my heart. Frequent chest pains and extreme shortness of breath reduced my tolerance for work. Furthermore, reoccurrence of the acute mucous colitis almost prostrated me. Longingly, I anticipated Arlene's arrival.

On July 10, 1973, Arlene arrived at the Tel Aviv Airport. When I saw her at a distance, I had this witness: "To you from failing hands I throw the torch. Be it yours to hold it high." Immediately, I knew Arlene was my God-given coworker. This would not be one year of volunteer work. Arlene would permanently serve God on the mission field. For no other person, except Elfrieda Greiner, had I received such a witness.

Three weeks after Arlene's arrival, I left her alone in Aboud while I traveled to Mexico City to attend the International Conference of Evangelism. During my absence, Brother Greiner, Elfrieda and Arlene completed plans for the dedication ceremonies for the new school.

On September 3, 1973, numerous friends from all over the country gathered again to celebrate the joyful dedication with us. Brother T.R. Morse, representing the Church of God World Missions Department, officiated at the ceremonies. There was quite a fanfare.

A fanfare of a different nature smoldered in silent preparation. The eruption came on Israel's highest holy day. While the Israelis fasted on Yom Kippur, the Arabs attacked, initiating the war of October 1973. Even in quiet Aboud we experienced the repercussions of this event.

Shortly before the Yom Kippur War, I was under the care of a gastro-intestinal specialist in Hadassah Hospital in Jerusalem. While I was undergoing an examination by that specialist, he prescribed an electrocardiogram that revealed that a heart attack was imminent. Before I could continue with any treatment, the hospital was filled with wounded soldiers from the Yom Kippur War, and the doctors were all mobilized.

My poor health caused Arlene grave concern, making her adjustment to the land and her work more difficult, but our adjustment to each other was the roughest of all.

Exact opposites, Arlene and I frustrated one another by almost everything we said or did or did not say or do. Fortunately, we could communicate and we both shared one unalterable objective—to adjust. Happily, we faced our problems with mature judgment, without playing any games. We tried sincerely to make any appropriate changes in our respective habits. It was certainly worth the effort. It would have been a pity to lose such a devoted, dependable and competent coworker as Arlene. Praise God! He made our adjustment possible.

As the church and school developed, the workload increased and the responsibilities multiplied. By early spring 1974, I was daily measuring my strength to the day's demands in hopes that I could come out even until the end of the school term. Alas, I came short of the demands.

In April 1974 while I was driving back to Aboud from Ramallah, I suffered a heart attack. For the remainder of the school year I could not return to school. He, who healed me of amoebic dysentery and acute mucous colitis, could raise me up also from a heart attack. And He would.

Chapter 15

EXCEEDINGLY
ABUNDANTLY MORE

*T*hroughout the summer of 1974 my mind struggled to adjust to my body's new limitations. Nothing that I had ever suffered had so radically affected my physical capacity as had the heart attack. Realizing that I could not command my accustomed responses, my mind and body had to work out a compromise whereby both could maintain maximum healthy activity. By taking much extra rest and keeping a positive mental attitude, my body regained much of its old vigor before the new term of school. Curriculum studies and teacher preparation for the new classes would take up all the time and energy I could muster while keeping up with all my regular duties.

Arlene and I shared the numerous janitorial and maintenance tasks. Our school children swept the school every

OF LIKE PASSIONS

day and mopped their classrooms once a week, but there were other rooms that the children did not touch. The teachers' lounge, library, science laboratory, office and toilets all had to be cleaned. Furthermore, the old school (transformed into a church annex), the church and the home combined with the school to make quite a lot of janitorial and maintenance chores.

Our school's playground was sticky red mud which packed into the hollow soles of the students' plastic sandals. Several times a day Arlene and I mopped up the adhesive mud from the halls and stairs where the children tracked it in.

Without knowledge of the Arabic language, Arlene was extremely limited in what she could do to assist me in anything related to administration in the school or in shopping for the school or home. She most adeptly developed the curriculum of her classes—English 3, 4, 5 and 6 and Physical Education 5 and 6. She graciously accepted the challenge to teach Arab children without knowing a word of Arabic—a challenge that has to be experienced to be appreciated. She joyfully helped in all the janitorial and maintenance duties, and she threw herself into intensive language study. All that activity while in the throes of her adjustment to the land, the people and to me, declared undeniably what a stable, devoted and competent coworker Arlene would be.

On the first day of the 1974-75 term, one of our teachers broke his contract. Many prospective teachers in Aboud village were seeking employment in our school, so it was not difficult to replace him. However, a totally untrained and inexperienced teacher presented a challenge.

To make the term more complicated, certain religious elements in Aboud, fearful of our growing influence, exhausted all possible measures to get our school closed. This opposition carried with it a blessing. The new Catholic priest, a pro-charismatic and beautifully cooperative Christian, stood firmly with us, making a united front

192

of Christian solidarity which discouraged opposition.

Two months after the opening of the 1974-75 term, the third-grade social studies teacher told me, "Sister, I have completed the social studies syllabus for grade three. What do you want me to do in this class the rest of the year?"

In startled disbelief, I wanted to cry out, "How could anyone ever exhaust the possibilities of teaching social studies." Fortunately, I controlled my surprise and thought it through.

Here was a 20-year-old peasant girl who had never been exposed to life beyond Aboud village. Her high school education had all been rote training from inadequate textbooks with no reference materials or teaching aids. In Aboud there were no newspapers, magazines, television, industry, commerce or transportation. How could she know about such things and all the social and economic influences they had on society and on the individual?

To make matters more complicated, the Ministry of Education provided us no textbooks for the course to give the teacher any guidelines. The only provision was a one-page outline that had to be developed into 110 lessons!

Swiftly, mentally making that evaluation, I realized the honest, naïve teacher had done all she could do. Calmly I asked, "When is your next social studies class scheduled?"

"On Monday morning, fourth period," came the reply.

"Then I'll discuss it with you on Monday morning before the opening of school," I said, dismissing her.

For two months I had been intensely occupied, giving basic instructions to our new teacher and preparing essential worksheets for her classes. Fortunately, I had a month's advance on that project. I dropped it temporarily and rushed to the rescue of the third grade social studies.

On Thursday morning, I wrote 110 lessons from the one page outline and the third grade social studies syllabus. I went to Jerusalem and bought pictures and collected materials from business establishments. Arlene helped me mount scores of pictures. Finally, I had bulletin board pictures as well as visual aids for each lesson. By Monday the lessons were filed in manila envelopes with their corresponding pictures and references to visual aids. Clearly marked on the outside of the envelope in Arabic and in English were the number and subject of the lesson and the enclosed materials.

Meeting the social studies teacher on Monday morning, I said, "When you told me on Thursday that you had completed the social studies syllabus for the year, I was really angry. Then I realized that I had no cause to be, so I didn't show it. Now, I have developed your syllabus for you so you have something to teach. If there is anything you do not understand about these materials, please do not hesitate to ask me."

Looking through the lessons briefly she exclaimed, "I'll never be able to cover all this material in one year!"

"I do not expect you to cover it all this year," I answered. "Begin at the very beginning and get as far as you can. Next year you can cover it all. I am not angry at you for not knowing how to develop this syllabus, but I shall be angry with you if you neglect using what has been developed for you."

For the following four years I would be making curriculum studies and writing textbooks for most of the classes. Worksheets and teaching aids had to be made. From class inspections and the subsequent observations of teachers' performances, I planned and presented teacher workshops. The results, which I did not know how to evaluate myself, obtained the highest evaluation of numerous local and foreign educators who visited our school. The director of education told me frankly that our school ranked highest in the West Bank. That is what the Lord wrought. May His name receive all the praise and glory!

After 33 years since my call to the mission field and 27 years in active mission service, I requested a year's leave of absence. Arlene was most efficiently assuming my head-mistress duties. The teachers were performing far above average. The relationships in our school were excellent and there was absolutely no discipline problem with the children. I could leave Aboud with no anxieties whatsoever concerning the administration of that mission station.

I had taken a total of only 17 months furlough in 27 years, and that had mostly been spent in deputation. My body and spirit demanded a prolonged rest. The World Missions Board granted the year's leave of absence, so I left Israel in time to arrive home for Christmas 1978.

My family generally thought that 27 years should be enough, and they begged me to consider staying at home. Various offers insuring my future security were advanced. Nothing, however, could erase the conviction that God had a greater plan for which I chose to wait and in which I chose to trust above all human propositions.

Along with waiting, my temporary rest also afforded me the chance to look back and reflect on my life up to that point. The rest of this chapter is the product of that reflection.

Looking back over all the years, have the efforts and the miraculous achievements been worthy of the total dedication of a human life? Has God's name been honored? Has His kingdom been served?

These are questions that many have asked me. Frequently, I have been told that my life has been wasted in that Middle East desert and that effort elsewhere could have produced more than that "handful of dry wheat."

By man's standard, my questioners have made good, logical conclusions. Aboud's church and elementary school—undeniably miraculous as they are to any honest critic—are small in the vast total Christian effort to evangelize our world. Any honest critic cannot deny that the combined total of all Christian effort to reach the nations with the good news of the gospel is sadly inadequate. If that is all God is doing, then His kingdom, as it is described in the Bible, will never come. If He is using only the Christians in His plan, many more millennia will probably not bring us closer to the reign of Christ on earth.

As I see it, God used Nebuchadnezzar and the heathen Babylonian Empire both as a disciplining rod for Israel and as a refuge to preserve the remnant while curing her of idolatry.

God used the Persian Empire and instigated the placing of Queen Esther for the purpose of sparing Israel and providing support for Israel to return and rebuild the temple in preparation for the Messiah.

God used the Greek and Roman empires to develop an international road network and extensive international language media in preparation for the propagation of the gospel message.

God used the Jewish persecution of the Christians to spur the Christians out of their cozy religious center and disperse them into all the world with the gospel as their security and their song.

I believe God uses any power or authority on Earth, whether they know it or not or whether they are willing or not. It is not imperative for me to comprehend how He is doing it. It is enough that I believe He is doing nothing less than working in ways that defy human reasoning to fulfill a plan that exceeds all human imagination, to bring His promised kingdom to pass. If I believe anything at all, I have to believe that the "kingdoms of this world are become the kingdoms of our Lord, and of his Christ; and he shall reign for ever and ever" (Revelation 11:15).

Sustained by this broadened concept, this glorious

vision, how do I conceive Aboud as fitting into the scheme?

What is Aboud? Who are the Aboud people?

Many people are satisfied to define Aboud as an insignificant Arab village on the occupied West Bank, too insignificant to merit a dot on most contemporary maps of the region. With only 3,000 population, it is situated on an isolated road away from all the economic centers. Quiet and mostly passive, it has not even merited any mention in all the political upheavals of the Middle East crises.

The Aboud people are common peasants. For many centuries they have not produced a leader of any import. Their language is Arabic. As for religion, half of the village is Islamic and half is Christian.

Is Aboud significant? Is it Arab? In the mind of God what is the identity of Aboud and its people?

In Old Testament times Aboud was situated on the main crossroads about 20 miles from Shiloh, once the religious and political center of the nation. It was 20 miles from Beth-el, 30 miles from Joppa, and 30 miles from Jerusalem. At its zenith, it had an estimated 40,000 population. Aboud, whose land still includes Timnath-serah, the place of Joshua's tomb, doubtlessly is the natural extension of that city as it moved nearer the Roman Highway, which was later constructed beside it.

In the Byzantine period, the fourth and fifth centuries of the Christian era, Aboud had seven established Christian churches, the ruins of which remain unto this day and one of which is used currently by the Greek Orthodox community. This means that the Aboud people were Christians from 200 to 300 years at least before the Arab invasion. It means that they were Christian at least 1,000 years before the Crusaders. Logically, one must deduce that Aboud's people were first century Christians. If so, are they Arab? Probably not. If they are not, who can they be? Are they

Jewish believers who escaped the Jewish persecution in Jerusalem and fled to the provinces? (See Acts 11:19) Are they a remnant of the Christians of Samaria converted under Philip's teaching? (See Acts 8:4-8)

I cannot speculate as to who they are, but I know Aboud and its people have had God's attention uniquely among all the villages of the West Bank. The gospel light has never been allowed to be extinguished completely in Aboud. Before the influences of one missionary completely die out, God sends another messenger to rekindle the gospel fires. Could it be that while my occupation with the church and the elementary school in Aboud holds me there, God is busy using powers and authorities far beyond my grasp to fulfill a more glorious design of which our church and school are only a minute part?

No satisfactory answer can be known but I believe in God and His kingdom. I know that the Lord Jesus Christ shall look on "the travail of his soul, and shall be satisfied" (Isaiah 53:11). The Child who was given to be Governor, Priest and Savior, shall not fail but shall bring salvation in all its connotations. The light of this truth has been kept before me in the lyric of an Irish song by William Fullerton, that I have written on the inside cover of my Bible. It reads:

"I cannot tell how he will win the nations,

How he will claim his early heritage,

How satisfy the needs and aspirations

Of east and west, of sinner and of sage.

But this I know, all flesh shall see his glory,

And he shall reap the harvest he has sown,

And some glad day his sun will shine in splendor

When he the savior, savior of the world is
known.

 I cannot tell how all the lands shall worship,

When at his bidding every storm is stilled,

Or who can say how great the jubilation,

When all our hearts with love for him are
filled.

But this I know, the skies will sound his
praises,

And myriad, myriad human voices sing,

And earth to heaven, and heaven to earth,
will answer,

At last the savior, savior of the world is king.

I rejoice that I have had and shall continue to have an
undefined part in God's kingdom. Eagerly, I anticipate the
future. It shall surely reveal, as has the past, God's exceedingly abundantly "more" than I could ask or think.

Chapter 16

WATERS UNDER THE PROVERBIAL BRIDGE

*I*t is October in Aboud but the year is 1999. Typically, summer's unrelieved heat unleashes its dying fury on the land. Every leaf and blade bend heavily under six month's accumulation of dust. The scorching east wind sucks moisture from your skin, leaving a deposit of sand in your hair, eyes and lungs. Villagers long for some rain to wash the trees so that the dust will not keep falling into their faces while they pick olives. It has not rained since the end of March; rain is long overdue. Nothing green remains in the fields. Dead briars and thistles twist around the stone boulders, making a trek to the trees more difficult. Trudging through deep sand filled with rolling stones grinds up shoes and strains leg muscles.

Overloaded cars and pickup trucks bringing olive pickers back from the distant fields have replaced the silent trains of bone-weary villagers and their patient donkeys of nearly two decades ago. The characteristic odors of the many commercial chicken houses have obliterated memories of the smoke from the taboon ovens. The installation of electricity in 1983 has opened up many labor-saving opportunities in the homes. Trucks loaded with used refrigerators, washing machines, television sets and other household furniture have been brought from Israel for sale in all the Occupied West Bank. For the first time, most of the villagers can sleep on beds or receive their guests on used sofas and armchairs. Work in Israel provides minimum wages which help the families to enjoy a sense of prosperity and relief.

During this time of relative prosperity many couples have married and settled in Aboud. Small two-room houses have sprung up throughout the village. Finally, they have paved the streets. It has been a time of real hope and contentment. Although it could not have been called an economic boom by any stretch of the connotation, the slight easing of dire poverty has birthed confidence in the future.

The economic changes have occasioned social changes. The customary, long evening visits with families and friends sitting on the floor exchanging small talk or news of the day have stopped. The men have to catch work buses long before dawn and ride one or more hours to their work places in Israel. The day of hard work and the bus ride home, even without undue road blocks, identity checks, and body searches, have left no inclination for any evening activities beyond family chores. On weekends, television has captivated its silent spectators, eliminating cheerful discussions.

In the past, when there were no diversions from the simple daily routine, engagements and, especially, weddings brought weeklong celebrations. Even though the bride received only the barest necessities and the groom often had to borrow an unpatched garment for the occasion, nothing dampened the enthusiasm. Singing, clapping and dancing carried on late every night. Now weddings last only two or three days, but brides are pampered with many gifts, jewels, beautiful wedding dresses, and trips for her and her attendants for full beauty treatments at the beauty salon. Grooms, too, dress in all new suits and provide "getaway" cars to not so distant or exotic honeymoon spots, usually for only one night.

In the past, when few families possessed any silverware, plates or even a table on which to use them, food was served on big round trays and everyone ate from the same trays with well-washed hands. This manner of eating by necessity carried over to the wedding feasts, where 400 or more guests shared the rice and meat meal. Now guests are provided with individual disposable plates, plastic spoons and forks, paper cups and napkins. Fruits, drinks and Arabic pastries improve the menu. There are more weddings, so no one could continue the strain of weeklong dancing for each bride.

Much of the economic and social changes are irreversible. The hope and confidence in the future, however, have received a near-fatal blow with the implementation of the Israeli Settlement Policy, which has sliced sizable portions of the Arab family properties to make room for Israeli towns and villages throughout the Occupied West Bank.

On December 9, 1987, a fight-to-the-death Arab uprising, called *Intifada*, erupted. Protests and counter protests from both sides of the conflict began in a mild way but escalated into inhumane, even gruesome acts, much of which dominated the news media from 1987 until the Oslo Peace Accords in 1994. Arlene and I experienced those years firsthand from a villager's point of view, but detailing it all is not the purpose of this narrative. What is important for this story is to understand its political, social and economical setting and the effects of the *Intifada* on our church and school.

Politically, the Settlement Policy was probably designed to insure Israeli security and control over the West Bank without annexing it, which could have been a bigger problem for Israel. The confidence that had been building between the Arabs and the Jews through work contracts and tentative interactions suffered severe cracks with Menachem Begin's Settlement Policy. Maybe that confidence could have been restored after the Camp David Peace Accords, in which Begin promised to freeze all settlement activity, had those promises been kept. Radicals from both sides kept peace at bay by exchanging petty insults that occasioned more serious incidents. These radicals were and remain a not-so-silent, even loud minority. With increasing tremors caused by violent acts, the cracked confidence finally shattered, plunging the West Bank and Israel into more than five years of total distrust with its spin-offs of eye-for-eye and tooth-for-tooth retaliations.

Economically, it was a disaster for both sides. War on any scale wastes the human resources and productivity of its perpetrators, not to mention property damage and causalities. Israel desperately needed the cheap but competent Arab labor to build for returning immigrants. The Arab West Bank provided easy markets for Israel's products. With continued cooperation the confidence could have grown. Maybe it would have even turned cordial. Unfortunately, Israel trusted in her military power and technology. She ignored the fact that the human spirit cannot be broken and that force breeds force. When the toll becomes too great to bear, an arbitrator is needed to help both sides return to sanity and cooperation.

Socially, the *Intifada* left its mark. It forced polarization of the Arabs between the left and the right. Arab youth took positions in varying extremes on both sides of the spectrum. This divided families and taxed churches in their efforts to accommodate the youth. Some parents watched helplessly, resorting only to constant prayer to keep their sons alive or out of prison.

Schools were disrupted first by students leaving class to demonstrate and throw stones. Then the Israeli army responded by requiring all schools to be closed by noon every day. Principals and faculty could not control the students, so the demonstrations and stone throwing continued. Furthermore, frequent strikes called by the leaders of the Intifada aggravated the situation from kindergarten to the college level. In response to the violence and the demonstrations, the Israeli authorities closed Bir Zeit University. Students, studying clandestinely from one secret location to another, took four years to complete a two-year program. The social fabric frayed, and the long-term results of the disruption of education will mark the Palestinians as surely as the Red Revolution left irreparable scars on China.

Resentment against our church and school increased during the *Intifada* for two reasons. As Americans, Arlene and I were suspected of pro-Israeli, anti-Arab sentiments. As much as possible, we did not strike or demonstrate. We concentrated on the business of educating the children and continuing the church ministries. We agreed that children in elementary school were too young to understand the politics and that they would serve themselves and their people better by staying in class and not striking or demonstrating.

My only role in the school at the time was to do the daily chapel. When I turned the school over to Arlene in February 1983, I returned to full-time church work.

In 1985 the Department of Education ordered the school to teach the Muslim religion. It could not be taught as a comparative religion by a non-Muslim. An imam or other Muslim teacher had to be allowed to teach it. Arlene and I agreed that there was no way we could teach Muslim religion in a Christian school. We knew that all the Christian schools on the West Bank had capitulated except two, but we felt it would be better to close the school than to allow Muslims to teach. It was a very difficult choice to make because we loved the Muslim children and their families. After prayer, the Lord directed us to send the students away with our blessing. This decreased the student body by one-half. The parents begged us to keep their children, but it was not our decision. Their government had forced the issue.

With the enrollment so low and the requirement to close the school at noon everyday, drastic changes had to be made in scheduling classes. Music, physical education, crafts and religion curricula were greatly curtailed in order to provide enough time for the core subjects, such as math, language skills and science. It was the best plan possible to minimize academic scars on the students.

Arlene obtained newly-published Sunday school workbooks that reinforced both Bible knowledge and language skills. To use the books, the students had to look up passages in the Scriptures, read with comprehension, answer questions, and do crossword puzzles and other exercises. Likewise, the girls clubs and the boys clubs had intensive programs that included crafts, physical activities, language skills and memorization.

I started Ladies Ministries (LM) the day I relinquished the school to Arlene. By the time the *Intifada* broke out, the ladies were meeting regularly. The weekly meetings gave me the opportunity to help our mothers focus on Christ, met the spiritual needs of the ladies, and provided them with a ministry to the children. The ladies held bazaars in which they sold their embroidery, jams, ketchup, potato chips, pickles and various novelties. They had used clothes sales, also. The ladies used all their resources to buy materials for the Blue Belles, the Joy Belles, the Young

Ladies Ministries (YLM), and the Christian Service Brigade.

Raika El Khoury, her nieces Mary and Hannie El Khoury, and Selwa Subhi completed the Girls Club Counselor Enrichment Training Course (CETC). Raika became counselor for the YLM;. Mary became counselor for the Joy Belles; and Selwa became counselor for the BlueBelles. Hannie went to Bible college in Bethlehem. These women translated the girls clubs' workbooks and used them to teach the children. When Selwa married Nihad Salman, and they became pastor of the Bethlehem Church of God, Hannie got permission to come to Aboud twice a month to direct the BlueBelles. Our girls and boys in their neat, beautiful uniforms impressed everyone, even the Israeli soldiers. The clubs ministered to the spiritual, social and academic needs of the children in those very hard times.

Raika was the first teacher I hired when I opened the school in 1970. Still a competent teacher, as well as a youth speaker, Raika has an important role with the LM. When our group outgrew the capacity of our available meeting room, I divided them into two groups: those up to 50 years old and those older. The combined group totaled 45 ladies. Raika took the younger group, in addition to her responsibility as a Sunday school teacher and counselor for the young ladies. She has taught most of the ladies in school at one time or another, so they greatly respect her wisdom and holiness. Through her teaching they learn how to pray, to trust God, to train their children, to love and honor their husbands, and to reflect Christ in their relationships with extended families and neighbors. Under Raika's leadership, five more ladies have earned the CETC certification: Somaya Issa, Clair Al Mualem, Suha Subhi, Naheel Azar and Lana Saleh. The ladies raised money to buy two church bells, and they contributed $1,000 for the new kindergarten and church ministries building. They paid for the kitchen cabinets in the church ministries part of the building. Today, the LM is very active with 58 members who serve the needs of the church and the school. They also reach out to the community.

January 16, 1991, the Gulf War convulsed the whole world. Aboud did not escape. Weeks before the first scuds fell on the land, all foreigners were urged to leave. The Church of God World Missions Department asked Arlene and me to leave. Nothing hindered her from leaving because she had only a temporary visa, but because I have a permanent residence visa, I was required to get an exit-reentry visa before I left. It took six days to process the visa, and I had to wait for it. In the meantime the war broke out.

The whole West Bank was clamped under a total curfew, which amounted to house arrest. Except for three brief breaks for the people to buy food, no one was allowed to go out into the yard or even on to the veranda for 42 days. Schools and churches were closed. It was not too uncomfortable for me. I was alone in two small rooms, a small kitchen and a bathroom; so, I was not cramped in my confinement. I had extra food since we had been warned of a possible missile attack. I had a gas mask, and a radio kept me informed of the scud attacks and when to enter or leave the sealed room. I had many tasks that I had been waiting to do. They occupied my time during the long days and nights.

The story was different for the Arabs. They lived in very crowded circumstances. Their houses were mostly as small or smaller than mine, and their families were big. I do not know how they managed to cope with grand–parents, parents, youth and small children closed inside for 42 days. Perhaps, only the visible scud missiles with the Patriots intercepting them over the immediate area, posing the threat of death by chemical warfare, kept the people focused on trying to survive.

Surviving a chemical attack was not the only concern.

For years the fathers had not been allowed to work in Israel. There were few opportunities for work on the West Bank, so food supplies were low. The family goats did not give milk at this time of year. While I enjoyed relative comfort and enough basic food, I could imagine the stress of the Aboud families compounded by their need for food.

Our LM had $200 in its treasury. I felt impressed to use the money to buy powdered milk for the families of our church and school. While I was wondering how to do this, I prepared vouchers for each family to take to the local grocery store to exchange for milk, but I did not know how to get the vouchers to the people or how to notify the store owner of my plan. I just had to wait.

After three weeks of total curfew, the Israeli army allowed the people to leave their houses for one hour to buy food and to see about their animals. In spite of pouring rain everyone went into the streets to see each other and to buy some provisions within the allotted hour.

From my apartment I could not see the street nor hear the loud commotion. Our church members pounded on my door and shouted, "Sister, we have one hour. Shouldn't we praise God for sparing us this far from chemical death?" I welcomed them in, and we had a prayer and praise service. We shared a portion of the Word to sustain us for whatever lay ahead.

I asked Raika and the ladies whether they agreed with me to use the LM money to buy milk for the church and school families. They were very happy to do it, so I gave them the vouchers to give out just before the curfew ended and they had to return home. Then, I called the owner of the store across the street from my house and asked him whether he could provide 46 gallon cans of Nido powdered milk. He said he would work on it. As owner of the store, he was given special permission to go to Ramallah to bring supplies for his store.

The next day someone knocked on my door. I was surprised because the curfew kept anyone from being out. When I opened my door, Paul Schmidgall, our overseer, had braved the curfew and had come to check on me. He had stopped his car a long way off and walked through the fields. I was overwhelmed and so glad to see him. He brought me my mail and some cheese, yogurt, margarine and fruit. I could not help crying for gratitude and the joy of seeing someone from outside and receiving news. Paul asked me if the people were in need and if we should help them. I told him about the vouchers that I had given for them to buy milk and about the money that paid for it. He said that he had received some money from Europe for relief, and he gave me back the $200!!! What a reason to keep me rejoicing for several days!

Raouf, the store owner, came to my door. He said that he had brought the milk and asked if I wanted him to bring it to my house. I told him to keep it at the store because the people would give him vouchers in exchange for the milk. I asked him to keep the vouchers and return them to me for receipts. When I asked him how much I owed him for the milk, I was surprised when he quoted me a price of $25 cheaper than I expected. When I asked him for an explanation, he answered: "Sister, if you are willing to buy milk for the needy people, I should at least bring it to the village at cost." This was the first crack in the hard heart of this man who had always opposed me and the church. I then asked if he could provide sacks of flour to be distributed by the same means. The money Paul gave me was enough for the flour.

Two days later we had another one-hour break in the curfew. Again, the people came to my house to pray and praise God that they were still alive. In spite of several scuds falling within two miles of Aboud, no one had been injured, and the scuds were not carrying chemical warheads. This was certainly sufficient cause to praise the Lord. After prayer, the people went to the store and got their milk. The next week they would get vouchers for flour.

Paul came back to check on me and he brought me mail, fruits, vegetables and dairy products. Again, I was overwhelmed by his caring and daring. He asked me again about the people's needs. I told him that they got the milk and that I had ordered sacks of flour for them with the money he brought me. So he gave me the money back again! We were able to spend the LM money three times because Paul gave us the contributions from Europe. The third time we gave out sacks of sugar.

The last time we had a break in the curfew the people were given two hours to be out of their houses. The rain that had lasted almost nonstop for the whole month gave way to cheerful sunshine. The people came to my door saying, "Sister, come quickly. We have two hours. It will be enough time to go to church. We can open the shutters and ring the bell and rejoice at God's great grace and keeping."

I was moved that the people always were delighted to use their short breaks in curfew to pray rather than to visit or walk the streets. We opened the shutters and rang the bell loudly and long. Then we had a wonderful service, even though it was not a church day.

The following week the war ended, and the curfew was totally lifted. We could return to school and church. Bright red poppies covered the fields. Almond trees blossomed everywhere. The heavy rains had brought new grass and edible plants. Happy to be outside, the ladies went to the fields to gather the greens for their families. Many baby lambs and kids worried their mothers as shepherds could finally lead them out to the hills. A nightmare had ended; a new day of hope had dawned. My staying there and Paul and the Europeans joining our ladies in providing for the people had turned the hearts of the people back to us. The anti-American feelings were greatly diminished.

Arlene was happy to return as soon as she could to finish the school term. We were still on short schedule. The *Intifada* did not end with the Gulf War. Frequently, graffiti covered the perimeter walls at the school, and the army forced Arlene to paint over it. The army presence was overpowering. Stone throwing resumed, but hostilities from the local population toward us eased.

On May 17, 1991, I left Israel for my regular furlough. My itinerary was planned for the whole summer. I looked forward to seeing many of our supporters again in their churches or in camp meetings. Unfortunately, those plans were cut short. I had a third heart attack and heart surgery. Arlene and Suhaila told me that all the churches and even the Muslims in Aboud prayed for my recovery. Friends and supporters from all over America prayed as well. Thank God, He restored me. I returned to Israel on February 13, 1992, and spent a few weeks with Arlene She left Israel for her furlough as soon as school was out for the summer.

On June 26, 1992, Butros and Mary Mualem, who had been studying at East Coast Bible College in Charlotte, North Carolina, returned to Aboud. Butros had been my assistant pastor for a full year before he married Mary El Khoury and they had gone away to college. As soon as they returned, they took over pastoring the Aboud Church of God, and they worked diligently in the youth camps.

With Butros and Mary pastoring the church, Raika heading up the LM, and Suhaila in charge of the school in Arlene's absence, my responsibilities were greatly diminished. It was an enormous pleasure to watch the national workers carry on so efficiently, but I had one more burden.

Butros and Mary did not have a place to live. I knew we could build a parsonage on top of the Aboud church. Just as I had built the school, I proceeded to build the parsonage - two bedrooms, an office, two baths, a kitchen and a great room. Alongwith the parsonage, I built a stairwell and a bell tower, and I renovated the front entrance to the church. When that was done, I felt that good provisions had been made for our trained Arab leaders. Seeing them work efficiently throughout 1992 and 1993, I decided that I was no longer needed in Aboud.

The doctors had warned me about sleeping alone in the village where we still had no telephone service or doctors and where the hospital was an hour's drive away. When Lambert DeLong, the Church of God superintendent of Eastern Europe and the Middle East, came for an official visit, I informed him and Paul that I would leave Israel when Arlene returned. I had already discussed this with Arlene before she went on furlough. I explained that the Arab workers had been trained and had proven themselves to be capable. It seemed right that they should be allowed to take over the work.

Brother DeLong asked me if I would stay in an advisory capacity if Arlene left. It made sense. I have a permanent residence visa, and I could stay at the Church of God on the Mount of Olives where there are three hospitals only five minutes away. He felt that Arlene could relocate and have a fruitful ministry elsewhere that she is much younger. I accepted his suggestion. Arlene was informed of the decision, and returned to Aboud to move her belongings. She was devastated. It was a very difficult time for everyone.

Under Suhaila's capable leadership, the enrollment of the school increased from 32 in 1993 to 121 in 1999. The Department of Education highly respects Suhaila and all of the teachers — Raika El Khoury, Somaya Issa, Miriam El Khoury, Rima Azar, Iftihar Salem, Layla Hameed, Hannie El Khoury, Senneh Shaheen and Mary Mualem. The Aboud Elementary School is rated as superior in all the Occupied West Bank.

In 1995 I started a day care center in connection with the Church of God on the Mount of Olives. At the same time, I was trying to plant a church in Jifna, a village between Jerusalem and Aboud. This was too much for me, especially since I was taking part in the services in Aboud and in Jerusalem. I returned late to Aboud on the Sunday afternoon of February 15, 1996, to take Raika, Suhaila and Clair back to the village. They, and sometimes others from the Aboud Church of God, helped me with singing and teaching in the Jifna mission. Feeling more tired than usual after three church services and more than 100 miles of driving in bad weather, I disregarded the warning of the doctors and slept that night in Aboud, alone in my apartment.

At 1:30 the following morning, I suffered a near-fatal fourth heart attack. I was not sure I would live until someone came to see about me. My landlord habitually made a tour around his house at 4:30 a.m. every day. Longingly, painfully, I waited for his round to call out to him for help. True to his habit, he came and found me. He ran to Butros and Mary for help. It was 6:30 a.m. before I arrived in Jerusalem at the hospital. Needless to say, it was too late for the treatment to save my heart from great damage.

I was in intensive care for 11 days and in the hospital a total of 22 days. My doctor lived in Ramallah, which is on the West Bank. During this time a suicide bomber blew himself up on a crowded Jerusalem bus. Immediately, the West Bank was sealed off, so my doctor could not get to Jerusalem to treat his patients at three hospitals. It was a novel experience to have my cardiologist treat me only by telephone, relying on the resident doctor's reports.

Besides my doctor not being allowed to reach me, I did not hear anything from World Missions for 10 days, as everyone was out of the office in special missions meetings at the time. Also, in the rush to get to the hospital I did not take any personal items, not even the telephone numbers of my family. Suhaila spent the whole first week with me night and day. When she returned to Aboud, I told her where to find the telephone number of my niece, Faith, and I asked her to call and inform my family of what was happening.

That same day I received a call from Faith saying that she was taking the first available plane to come and take me home. What a comfort it was to hear her voice! Two days later Christopher Moree called me and assured me that World Missions had been praying for me and that they were ready to do anything I needed. It was only after I received those calls that I realized how lonely and isolated I had felt. Suhaila's presence and the care of Ossman Ali and Hanne, his wife, had filled the gap, but nothing takes the place of family in times like those.

True to her word, Faith came on the earliest flight, and she brought a round-trip ticket for me. She relieved Suhaila and slept with me in the hospital until the day I left. As soon as she could get my exit-reentry visa, she brought me home on March 21, 1996. Intensive treatment, cardiac-rehabilitation and much rest barely kept me going. Finally, in December I underwent bypass surgery. The fact that the church and the school in Aboud was carrying on with no problems under the Arab leadership gave me peace of mind, making recuperation easier. On my first trip back to Aboud, Faith moved all my belongings to one room in the Mount of Olives Church of God in Jerusalem. I have never spent a night alone in Aboud again.

The Department of Education began to insist that we move the kindergarten out of the elementary school building into an independent place. There was and still is a great housing shortage in Aboud, so we could not rent anything. We did not have land on which to build. That changed in October 1997. Our neighbor decided to sell us the lot that joins our school. He would not sell it to anyone but me. I could not get a flight to Israel until November 20. Paul Lauster, the regional superintendent for Mediterranean and the Middle East, and his wife, Lilli, were in Israel for church business. In December we met with Abu Samira, the owner of the land for sale, at the land registry office in Ramallah and finalized the sale of his lot to the Church of God. Suhaila had all the school children to make Christian flags which they pasted on long cords. When we returned to Aboud from buying the land, she arranged a big party to celebrate the acquisition. We took our big Christian flag and all the flags that the children had made and went next door to the newly-acquired lot and dedicated it to the kingdom of God. The children's flags remained strung from tree to tree as we returned to the school rejoicing.

Back in America on December 22, I worked diligently to prepare a project proposal to present to the Department of Ladies Ministries in hopes that they would build a kindergarten and church ministries building for us.

Why a church ministries building? The landlady of the apartment that I had rented for more than 30 years asked us to vacate the apartment because her grown son needed to renovate it and live in it when he married. They had a right to get the apartment back, but we had no place to move. The church used the apartment for 13 ministries. How could we continue the ministries? Where would they store their materials?

By building a three-story building with the top floor being completely separated from the two lower floors, we could make the top floor available to the church ministries and have two independent floors for the kindergarten. Such an arrangement seems ludicrous to those who do not understand how small our land is. In Israel and in the West Bank one cannot build ranch-style buildings. Our whole property is only one-half acre. We have to build up or not at all.

Unfortunately, the Ladies Ministries Department had already accepted their projects through the year 2000, and they could not accept our project. Pressured by the Department of Education, by the landlady of our church annex, and by the parents of 50 Muslim children who were begging us to take their children into our kindergarten, an urgency existed that I could not ignore. Again, I undertook to build by faith.

Waters Under the Proverbial Bridge

In March 1998 I was guest speaker for the Men and Women of Action Rally in Sevierville, Tennessee. Going back to Sevierville was a real pilgrimage for me. It was there that I received my call to the mission field. It was there where God began to teach me the wonders and delight of relying on Him to provide for all my needs for spirit, soul and body.

I took my audience on a mental pilgrimage. I shared the incredibly tender stories of my heavenly Father's guidance and provision and how those experiences captivated me and led me to the ends of the earth in a joyful and total abandonment which holds me in its grip until this hour. I shared my burden and the need for building the kindergarten and church ministries facility in Aboud without any delay. I thanked them for building the lovely house for me in Pell City, Alabama, where I was just beginning to experience the luxuries of central heating and a bed long enough to accommodate my feet and ankles. I promised them that I would willingly and without hesitation sell the new house to finance a building for the ministries in Aboud. The vision of evangelizing the world in direct obedience to Christ's last command takes priority over my living the rest of my life in comfort in this wonderful land.

In response to my sharing my heart and vision, the 200 Men and Women of Action who were present gave $60,000 in cash and pledges They promised to send a team of workers to Aboud in October to work on the building. This was absolutely a confirmation to me that God was in the plans and that He was providing.

I went back to Israel and stayed from May until mid-July to get the preliminaries done and to get the actual building started. The first footings were poured on July 11, 1998. The Men and Women of Action team arrived late in the night of October 25 and worked from the very next day through November 6. The work continued, using paid local labor. By December the church ministries could vacate the church annex apartment and move into the first floor of the new building. Work continued on the two upper floors as fast as possible in an effort to have the building ready for the opening of school in September. Enforced building codes that did not exist when the first school was built increased the price of the building to over $200,000 dollars. I did not have to sell my house, but I borrowed $21,000 to keep the project on track. I also gave my life insurance policy to pay for the debt in case of my sudden death - which is more than a possibility.

By the time for school to start in September 1999, all the floors were in use. At Thanksgiving, the whole church community and friends joined in our traditional Thanksgiving Day celebration on the top floor. More than 200 worshippers thanked God for providing for the kindergarten and church ministries.

On my last visit to Aboud in March 1999, I looked out over the church, the original school building, the parsonage, and this fine new building and asked God, "How did it all happen? From where did all of this come?"

He spoke to me and said, "You did it."

"Now God," I answered, "anyone with common sense or uncommon sense would know that an unsophisticated 20-year-old Alabama girl who left America with only two years of college, little experience and no money could never have achieved such results. What do you mean?"

"You did it," He said again. "By trusting me enough to stay in my workshop, producing piece by tiny little piece of confusing and seemingly totally unrelated parts over many years, you did it for me. And I assembled it."

I believe what God said to me, and yet I still ponder the lifelong process, especially the 36 years in Aboud. I know there were many key people who had a part in it all. I know I could have done nothing without blind Zarefie

Saleh, whose prayers to God for a resident missionary and her invitation to me to come to Aboud started it all. She opened her one-room house for services. She interpreted for me for 15 years in church, Sunday school and weekly visitations, and for Arlene for another 12 years with no salary.

I could have done nothing permanent or effective without the full support of Muallam Ibrahim who was already 100 years old when I arrived in Aboud. He had been in the ministry in the Anglican church, working with their missionaries since his youth and had suffered imprisonment for the gospel before the outbreak of World War I. Like Zarefie, he longed to see the continuity of the Protestant mission in Aboud. Without the sanction of this venerable family head, nothing I could have done would have had credibility. One does not build churches with children in Arab lands. God gave us a patriarch who passed his torch to me, thus opening the door for anyone in his tribe to enter.

I could have done little without Abu Majid, who followed in Muallam Ibrahim's footsteps and assumed the family patriarchal role when Muallam Ibrahim died. Abu Majid, on behalf of his father and his siblings, donated the land on which we built the church. He was my defender and a faithful backbone of the church as long as he lived.

Arlene Miller came to Aboud nine years after I arrived, and three years after I started the Aboud Elementary School. She worked efficiently and willingly in any capacity, whether it was menial labor or highly sophisticated employment in the school and youth work for which she had special gifts. She taught school, developed the English and math curricula, prepared the layout of the girls clubs' workbooks for publication, and coordinated the Sunday school lessons with the school religion classes so that there would be no overlap in subject matter. She bought the Sunday school workbooks and briefed the teachers on how to use them and kept them carefully filed for future use. The menial jobs were too many to list. She and I worked together to maintain the buildings in order to save all the contributions to pay the teachers.. Arlene's work of 20 years is still much appreciated. I did not do more than she.

Our efforts would have been greatly hindered without cheerful, competent teachers. For decades they have been willing to work, study and grow as they taught. They always cooperated and never had quarrels.

Raika and Suhaila have been key instruments of God. Each of them has contributed more to the Aboud Church of God and the Aboud Elementary School than I have in terms of loyal work. They are currently holding everything together with the help of God in these trying times. They are wonderful unsung gems and a credit to the ministry.

What could I have done without faithful prayer partners of nearly five decades? Their names would make a list too long to include in this manuscript.

This whole wonderful mission has been supported mostly by donors who gave $10 a month. A few gave 20 and even fewer gave more. The school has never been in the World Mission's budget. Until now, it is a faith undertaking. All who have given the smallest or the biggest contributions over the years are not nameless or unknown to heaven, which reserves a rich reward for each of them. Whatever I have done was made possible by their support.

It goes without saying that I, who left home with nothing at the age of 20, had nothing to give financially. The precious supporters trusted me to be faithful in channeling the gifts they gave to me, and I have felt the burden of accountability to do that almost to a fault. I hope that those who come behind me will be satisfied that I have done that. It is more than obvious that I could have done nothing without my beloved supporters.

What, then, was my part? I believe what God said, but what does it mean? Maybe I was a voice crying in the wilderness. Maybe I was a prophet digging ditches in the desert. Maybe I was, and am still, an insatiable lover of God and His people and purpose. Maybe, in some indiscernible way, I was permitted to be a catalyst. All the questions remain. In the final analysis I am still only a woman "of like passions" as anyone who reads this story.

OF LIKE PASSIONS

Margaret Gaines

Missionary to the Arabs

Photo Gallery

(Above) Margaret as a baby (1932) ready to face the world.

(Above) Margaret's parents with her older siblings, Ruth, Paul and Florence.

(Above) This 1943 photo shows Margaret surrounded by her siblings; from left to right: Ollie, Ada, Margaret, Velma and Paul.

(Above) Margaret, who is 5-years old here, stands beside her older sister, Ollie.

(Left) In front of the Anniston home, Mama Floy (Margaret's step-mother) is surrounded by Margaret and Paul on the left, and Ada and her husband, Johnie, on the right. This was Margaret's 14 year—the year she gave her life to Christ.

(Below) Margaret is greeted by Josephine Planter upon Margarets' arrival in Tunisia to serve with this veteran missionary.

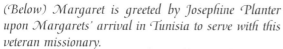

(Above) Margaret's passport photograph in 1952, when she sailed to Tunisia.

(Below) Students in the school in Tunis, Tunisia in 1960.

(Left) Margaret with some of her "Children" in front "Garage" church in Megine, Tunisia in 1954.

(Left) A portrait of Margaret in 1956 during her time as Missionary in Tunisia.

(Above) Zarefie Saleh, whose blindness did not keep her from envisioning the answer to her prayer that God would send a Christian missionary to Aboud. God sent Margaret Gaines, who began her Mission in Zarefie's one-room house.

(Above) This is the one-room house where Zarefie Saleh lived with her mother and father and in which Margaret began the Aboud Mission.

(Left) Arab children from the village of Aboud.

(Above) Muallam Ibrahim was the family patriarch who "opened the door" to the Arab mission in Aboud. He was over one-hundred years old when Margaret first came to Aboud.

(Above) Abu Majid, Zarefie Saleh's brother, was one of Margaret's converts and he became the leading patriarch of th Aboud Mission after Muallem Ibrahim.

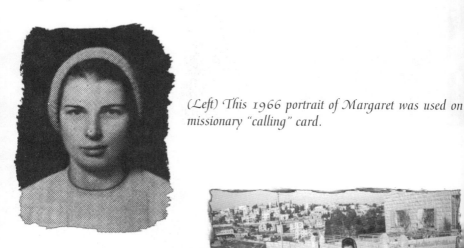

(Left) This 1966 portrait of Margaret was used on missionary "calling" card.

(Right) Margaret stands beside her "beetle", which received "not a scratch" during its strategic use in the 6-Day War in 1967.

(Left) Kevin was Margaret's "best friend" during isolated moments of the 6-Day War.

(Right) A portrait of Margaret in the early Aboud years.

(Left) Congregation of the Aboud Church of God at the dedication service in 1969.

(Right) The original Aboud Church of God, dedicated in September 1969.

(Left) The Aboud Church of God was expanded in the Summer of 1992, with the construction of a new parsonage and bell tower.

(Below) Members of the Aboud Children's Clubs standing in front of the newest building under construction.

) The teachers at the Aboud Elementary School. Left to right
row): Iftehar, Mary, Somaya, Reema, Aida, Laila, Raika, Suhaila
ow): Margaret Gaines, Arlene Miller.

) Margaret in native Arab dress, as
at the 1996 Church of God General
oly in Indianapolis, Indiana.

(Above) Margaret Gaines, in the
231 Summer of 1999.

This portrait, featuring Margaret surrounded by faces representing her Arab "fami[ly]" was painted by Tom Rosson, who was a fellow classmate during Margaret's Lee Coll[ege] years.